VOLUNTEERING AND SOCIETY

Editors

Rodney Hedley has extensive experience of volunteering and the voluntary sector. Formerly research officer at the Centre for Policy on Ageing and at the London School of Economics, he was head of the London Neighbourhood Care Action Programme for three years. He writes regularly on voluntary sector matters.

Justin Davis Smith is head of research at The Volunteer Centre UK. He has wide experience in conducting and managing research and is editor of 'Voluntary Action Research', a series of papers on volunteering issues. He was previously research assistant to the Rt Hon Sir James Callaghan, MP (now Lord Callaghan) and is the author of *The Attlee and Churchill Administrations and Industrial Unrest, 1945–55*, published by Pinter Press in 1990.

Contributors

Peter Ely is lecturer in social work at the University of Kent at Canterbury; David Obaze is national development officer of the Resource Unit to Promote Black Volunteering; Colin Rochester is research development officer at the Centre for Voluntary Organisation, London School of Economics; Jos Sheard is principal officer (volunteers) with the London Borough of Croydon; Mai Wann was responsible for setting up the National Self-Help Support Centre and currently works as a consultant; and Elaine Willis is deputy director of The Volunteer Centre UK.

VOLUNTEERING AND SOCIETY

Principles and Practice

**Edited by Rodney Hedley
and Justin Davis Smith**

Published by
BEDFORD SQUARE PRESS of the
National Council for Voluntary Organisations
26 Bedford Square, London WC1B 3HU

First published 1992
© Rodney Hedley and Justin Davis Smith, 1992

Typeset by Contour Typesetters, Southall, London
Printed and bound in Great Britain by Redwood Press Ltd,
Melksham, Wilts

Cover printed by The Heyford Press, Wellingborough

A catalogue record for this book is available from the British Library

ISBN 0 7199 1315 2

Contents

Preface

We began discussing the need for this book in September 1988. From our work with volunteer organisers and policy makers, we knew that they wanted to know 'more' about volunteering. While we could refer them on to numerous research reports and articles we were aware that a comprehensive text on volunteering, or the issues it raised, was not available. We felt that a publication was wanted to fill the gap and the idea for *Volunteering and Society* was born.

An idea is one thing; reality is another. We began to discuss the subject matter which such a book might contain. This took many months and consultations with many people. Volunteering permeates all aspects of our daily life, and all activities. We were sure about some of the contents of the proposed book – that came from the enquiries to us. But what else should we cover? We knew that we could slice the cake in many ways, and thus discussed numerous outlines.

By the end of 1989 we had emerged with the book you have here. As we commissioned authors, we realised that the need for such a book was as strong as ever. Volunteering has a national profile more prominent than ever before and it is now appearing in political party programmes. In 1990 the report on Citizenship by the Speaker's Commission was published and Prince Charles launched his volunteer youth scheme. Community care is a greater issue than ever before as health and social services are revolutionised by the National Health Service and Community Care Act.

Our book intends to help people working with volunteers to have a better understanding of the role of volunteering in society. As well as covering policy issues, we hope that there is also enough practical advice within the text.

We thank Bedford Square Press of the National Council for Voluntary Organisations for encouraging us with the idea, and our contributors for making the book so interesting, thought-provoking and lively.

The views expressed in *Volunteering and Society* are those of individual contributors, and are not necessarily those of NCVO.

Introduction

Rodney Hedley and Justin Davis Smith

The Challenge for the Volunteer Movement

Volunteering is vital and relevant to all of us. But, as we go into the 1990s, volunteering is in a state of flux. The last decade has seen a massive increase in the demand for volunteers, the result of both government policy and changing values in society. At the same time, there is evidence of a crisis in the recruitment of volunteers. Some organisations are experiencing a shortage of volunteers because of changes in the population structure and in the workforce. There is a growing crisis of identity as government monopolises the ethos and language of the volunteer movement. Major questions are being asked of voluntary action and its value. Commentators, such as Stuart Hall, have argued that the volunteer movement is in danger of losing its independence.

The challenge for the volunteer movement is to repond to these crises in order to ensure that volunteering remains vital and relevant, into this decade and beyond.

A Crisis of Supply

Evidence shows that many organisations are finding it difficult to recruit and hold on to volunteers. Volunteering is being severely affected by both demographic trends and changes in the structure of the paid workforce.

Demographic Trends Affecting Volunteering

The fall in the birth rate since the late 1960s means that there are fewer

young people available to volunteer. Youth organisations in the UK
are experiencing acute shortages of volunteers. Alongside the fall in
birth rates, we have an increase in the numbers of elderly people in
society. In 1971 there were 7.5 million people aged 65 or over. By 1986
the figure stood at 8.7 million. By 2001 it is estimated that there will be
over 9 million people in the 65–plus age bracket. This is likely to affect
volunteering in two ways. Data show that older people are under-
represented as volunteers, so we would expect fewer volunteers. A
survey carried out by Social and Community Planning Research
(SCPR) for The Volunteer Centre in 1981 showed that only 12 per
cent of regular volunteers are aged 65 or over.[1] At the same time, the
increasingly elderly structure of society will lead to an increase in
demand for volunteers in the health and social welfare field. So there
will be a fall in supply at the same time as an increase in demand.

Economic Changes Affecting Volunteering

The entry of more women into the paid labour market means that
fewer women are available to do voluntary work. A number of
voluntary organisations which rely almost exclusively on female
volunteers, such as the Women's Royal Voluntary Service and the
Red Cross, are facing severe recruitment problems. This trend looks
set to continue as falling birth rates and the tightening labour market
lead employers to attempt to attract married women back into the
paid labour market.

Continuing high levels of unemployment in many parts of the UK
are accentuating the problems of volunteer recruitment as evidence
shows that unemployed people are less likely to volunteer than people
in paid work.

Social Trends

In addition to demographic and economic changes, there are long-
term social trends which are having an adverse effect on volunteering.
The break up of traditional family structures is one such development.
We know that married people are more likely to volunteer than single
people. Single people make up only 10 per cent of regular volunteers,
according to the 1981 Volunteer Centre Survey. The increase in
divorce rates and the move away from 'traditional' family structures
thus has its effect on volunteer levels.

The break up of traditional 'close-knit' communities also has its impact on volunteering. The increase in personal and occupational mobility over the last 25 years has resulted in a decline of traditional communities. People are spending more time outside their neighbourhoods, both for work and leisure. Consequently, there is less opportunity for community bonding and less opportunity for neighbourhood activity.

At the same time, there is a trend towards the 'privatisation' of home life. People are not only spending less time within their communities, but are spending more time within the confines of their own home – a trend likely to continue with the spread of in-house entertainment, such as videos and cable and satellite TV. Again this will limit the opportunity for voluntary activity.

Set against the changes we have looked at, there are positive trends affecting volunteering. The long-term trends towards a shorter working week, more part-time work and job-sharing initiatives, and the move towards earlier retirement will give people more time to undertake voluntary work (although the trend towards earlier retirement is currently being reversed due to the tightening of the labour market). Increased public awareness of green issues has led to a rapid expansion of environmental volunteering in recent years. However, the general picture is one of a growing crisis of recruitment in volunteering.

A Crisis of Identity

There is a second crisis in volunteering today, which can be termed a crisis of identity. In many ways, this second crisis is more worrying than the fall in volunteer numbers as it threatens the very existence of the volunteer movement as an independent social movement. This crisis of identity has been most clearly spelt out by Professor Stuart Hall of the Open University in *The Voluntary Sector under Attack?*[2]

Hall's thesis is that the volunteer movement is in danger of being taken over, or 'colonised' by the new welfare ideology brought about by the Conservative governments of the 1980s, not in any absolute sense of ownership but in the ownership of ideas and philosopy. The last 10 years in the UK has seen what Hall describes as a concerted attack by the government on the welfarism of the postwar years, on what has been termed the 'culture of dependency' and the 'nanny state'. And the vigorous pursuit of policies based on a contrary philosophy – one of self-reliance, consumer rights, economic efficiency and de-regulation.

The government's attack on the 'disabling' institutions of the welfare state and the emphasis on self-reliance and consumer rights, echo the 'grass-roots' and self-help movements of the 1960s and 1970s that did much to shape the volunteer movement of today. The volunteer movement has also been critical of state welfarism for being over-bureaucratic, out of touch and unresponsive to change.

So, is the New Right talking the same language as the volunteer movement? Are government calls for increased reliance on charity and volunteers in line with the ideals and philosophy of the volunteer movement? Hall argues that it is not. He claims that the government is stealing the language of the volunteer movement – the language of self-help and consumer rights – in pursuit of its own philosophy of economic liberalism and of rolling back the frontiers of the state. Government calls for an increase in voluntary activity, in this view, have more to do with nineteenth-century views of philanthropy and charity than with the ideals and philosophy of the volunteer movement today.

According to Hall there have been 'four great movements', in addition to Victorian philanthropy, that have helped to shape the volunteer movement. The first of these movements was the collapse of 'doctrinal laissez-faire', that is, the rigid belief in non-interference by the state, as a result of the failure of private charity to cope with the poverty and squalor of the Victorian age. The second movement was the gradual extension of citizenship (in terms of civil, political and economic rights, as well as legal rights) to all members of society – a process that is still incomplete. The third movement was the institutionalisation of these changes in the great 'welfare experiment' of the postwar years. The fourth stage in the development of the volunteer movement was the great upsurge in 'grass-roots', community-based organisations in the 1960s and 1970s, which were partly a response to what were widely seen as the failures of the welfare state. Of special importance was the growth of mutual aid and self-help groups which moved away from old notions of charity and dependency. In the self-help group, people come together to help themselves and other people – the old stereotype of volunteering as charity and dependency begins to break down. Mutuality and plurality are the key words.

It is this emphasis on mutual assistance and reciprocity which is in danger of being undermined by government colonisation of the volunteer movement. For the government, volunteering is about the well-to-do giving assistance to those in need. It is the language of charity and dependency, not of mutual assistance and citizenship.

A Response to the Crisis in Volunteering

How should organisations best respond to this dual crisis in volunteering: the crisis of supply and the crisis of identity?

There are two steps which need to be taken in response to the crisis. First, organisations need to widen the base from which they recruit volunteers in order to reflect more fully the heterogeneous nature of society. Second, the volunteer movement needs to rediscover its identity, to begin, as Hall puts it, to 'articulate and develop a new kind of public culture, a new conception of welfare'.

Widening the Base of Volunteering

The stereotype of a volunteer as a middle-aged, middle-class woman has never been entirely true. Volunteering is open to all people in society and all types of people volunteer – to some extent. Nevertheless, it is the case that volunteering is linked to socio-economic position, age and gender. Fewer people from lower socio-economic groups volunteer; fewer young people and people over the age of retirement volunteer; fewer men volunteer; and fewer people from ethnic minorities volunteer. The crisis in supply of volunteers provides the much-needed push for organisations to reach out to those groups in society which are under-represented as volunteers.

Such a policy will not be easy: there will be increased costs in recruitment, in the provision of specialist training and in the support of new volunteers. But it will be time and money well spent. Without the injection of new volunteers, many groups will find it difficult to survive over the next few years. This is quite apart from the benefits to the organisations and to the individuals concerned of opening up volunteering to all in society.

Rediscovering its Identity

The widening of the base of volunteering will help the volunteer movement to rediscover its identity and to develop a new 'public culture'. This culture should start from the premise that volunteering is open to all. It should stress that volunteering is no longer (if it ever was) about charity and dependency, but is about mutual support and reciprocity. The new public culture of volunteering should stress the value of volunteering to the volunteer himself or herself. It should stress the important role of volunteering as self-help. It should stress the role of volunteering as advocacy and as campaign work, and not just as service delivery in the health and personal social services. The new public culture of volunteering should welcome government attempts to encourage voluntary activity, through such initiatives as the Active Citizen campaign, but should point to the deficiencies of a view which equates volunteering with charity and good works.

By making volunteering more relevant, more accessible and more democratic this new public culture will help reverse the trend of a reduction in the number of volunteers and better equip the volunteer movement to face the challenges of the next decades.

Structure of the Book

In this book, we examine some of the issues facing the volunteer movement today. Our approach has been to start with the contexts of volunteering in the UK and in mainland Europe in Part 1, and then to focus on current issues in Part 2. We have had to leave some important topics out: volunteering in community care, the environment, for people with learning difficulties, and the media to name a few. We apologise, and hope that another book will be written.

Definition

As the chapters show, volunteering can take on different meanings. Traditional definitions of volunteering have focused on three elements: the gift of time; the element of free choice; and the lack of payment. For example, The Volunteer Centre in 1983 defined volunteering as 'work undertaken on behalf of self or others outside the immediate family; not directly in return for wages; undertaken by free choice; not required by the state or its agencies'.[3]

Developments in the past few years have undermined this traditional definition. The spread of 'paid volunteering' schemes, especially in the field of community care, has broken down the rigid delineation between paid work and voluntary work. Volunteer initiatives in schools and the workplace, the increased use of community service orders and moves towards American-type work-fare systems show that voluntary activity is not always freely entered into.

This book contributes to the debate about shifting boundaries and definitions. It adopts a broad definition of volunteering, looking at activity in both the voluntary and statutory sectors. It examines self-help as a form of volunteering. It looks at volunteering arranged in an informal way, but is not about informal help or care of the kind given to relatives.

Contexts

In Part 1 on contexts, we start with 'Volunteering and Society,' Jos Sheard's account of how volunteering has shaped, and been shaped, by government policy in the postwar period. We see how volunteering was seen as a palliative to youth problems in the 1960s; as a way to deliver social services in the 1970s; and as a sop to unemployment in the 1980s. Jos ends with a discussion of recent government attitudes towards volunteering, including active citizenship. In 'An Uneasy Alliance', Justin Davis Smith explores the history of relations between volunteers and trade unions, and points to the development of a 'new partnership' between paid and unpaid workers. Peter Ely, in 'Democracy, Voluntary Action and the Social Welfare Sector in Mainland Europe', introduces us to the context of volunteering in a number of European countries. Peter's thesis is that volunteering is necessary for a healthy democratic development. You will read with interest about how volunteering was used in pre-glasnost Soviet Russia. Justin ends the section with 'What We Know About Volunteering', a brief look at the research evidence on volunteering, noting definitions and participation rates.

Current Issues

Part 2 on issues begins with Rodney Hedley's chapter 'Organising and Managing Volunteers'. He considers motivation for volunteering and the constant dilemma that volunteer organisers have of reconciling organisational objectives and volunteer needs. The chapter ends with a checklist on good practice. In 'Community Organisations and Voluntary Action', Colin Rochester examines volunteering and community development. He shows how informal volunteering operates, and how important it is to local community activity and democracy. As in other forms of participation in British society, black people have been ignored or side-tracked. David Obaze explores the growth of black volunteering and black voluntary action in 'Black People and Volunteering'. Elaine Willis, in 'Volunteers as Advocates', considers what is an important but often-neglected role of volunteers. This advocacy role is more vital than ever given the complexity of everyday living, and the control which professionals have over us. Finally, Mai Wann brings us back to the heart of volunteering in a discussion of self-help groups. In 'Self-Help Groups: Is there Room for Volunteers?' she discusses the ideological roots of self-help and looks at the relationship between self-help groups, and volunteers and professionals.

PART ONE

CONTEXTS

CHAPTER 1

VOLUNTEERING AND SOCIETY, 1960 to 1990

Jos Sheard

The Volunteer Boom

Before the 1960s, voluntary work in the UK was more or less synonymous with philanthropic work on behalf of charitable and voluntary organisations, generally carried out by middle-class or upper-class people of middle age. The stereotyped image was that of the 'Lady Bountiful'. There were also vigorous traditions of working-class self-help and mutual aid, based on such networks as trade unions and friendly societies – though these would seldom have been recognised, by those involved, as 'volunteering'. After the foundation of the welfare state in the late 1940s, these traditional volunteers found themselves somewhat sidelined, as the National Health Service and local government welfare services expanded to take over many of the activities previously carried out on a voluntary basis. However, the 1960s saw a major revival of interest in volunteering, accompanied by a marked change in public perceptions of volunteers and their role in society.

This was partly prompted by a change of attitude towards the welfare state. Beveridge himself had pointed out at the inception of the welfare state in 1948, in his report, *Voluntary Action*, that collective action by the state alone would not be sufficient to eradicate the 'Giant Evils' of Want, Disease, Ignorance, Squalor and Idleness from society. He had argued that there would be a continuing need for individual voluntary effort to complement the services of the welfare state.[1] Nevertheless, there was a general assumption in the 1950s that from now on, professional workers in the statutory services would meet all the needs. But once it became apparent, after the welfare state had been in operation for a decade or so, that the professionals were not able to meet all the needs – and that sometimes their methods could be rather too remote and bureaucratic – interest revived in the contribution which volunteers might be able to make.

Volunteers, it was thought, might be a useful way of remedying some of the deficiencies which people had begun to perceive in the welfare state. They would be a source of extra labour to help meet some of the shortfalls in the overall level and pattern of service delivery – thus supplementing statutory services. In addition, they might make up for some of the shortcomings in the quality of publicly run services, by bringing a more personal touch and an element of community participation to otherwise bureaucratic organisations – thus complementing statutory services.

One result of the reawakened interest in volunteering was that the National Health Service embarked on a programme of promoting volunteer involvement in hospitals throughout the country. From 1962 onwards, the Ministry of Health issued a series of Circulars giving guidance on the recruitment, placement and support of volunteers, and on the appointment of paid voluntary service co-ordinators.[2] The first two VSCs were appointed in 1963, at Fulbourn Hospital, Cambridge, and St Thomas's Hospital, London.

Official enthusiasm for volunteering was also reflected in a succession of reports published throughout the 1960s:

- the Newsom Report (1963) advocated community service by schoolchildren as part of the school curriculum[3]
- the Bessey Report (1966) led to the foundation of Young Volunteer Force Foundation[4]
- the Reading Report (1967) recommended the use of volunteers in the Probation Service[5]
- the Seebohm Report (1968) argued that volunteer recruitment would be a key task for the proposed new social services departments[6]

Changing attitudes towards the welfare state, however, were not the only reason for the revival of interest in volunteering in the 1960s. The other main factor was concerned with changing attitudes towards young people. From the late 1950s onwards, the problem of the generation gap began to enter the popular consciousness and established adult society began to be increasingly alarmed at what it perceived as anti-social behaviour by a succession of youth sub-cultures. The Teddy Boys and Beatniks of the 1950s gave way to the Mods, Rockers, Hippies, Hell's Angels and student revolutionaries of the 1960s. The newspapers and television regularly gave prominent and sometimes sensational coverage to scenes of violence and disorder involving groups of young people. Such events, whether involving Mods and Rockers on the beach at Margate or anti-war protesters in Grosvenor Square, became lumped together in the minds of the adult public as indications of an imminent breakdown in the fabric of society. 'Your sons and your daughters', sang Bob Dylan, 'are beyond your command.' The events in Paris in May 1968 heightened this anxiety still further, seeming to reawaken the spectre of revolution spreading from across the Channel. The feeling of the establishment of the time was expressed very clearly by Dr H.M. Holden, in his foreword to Tim Dartington's book on Task Force: 'Small wonder that the older generation feels threatened and tends to use adolescents as scapegoats, especially when confronted with organised movements such as the Hippies and, more recently, the left-wing students' rebellion.'[7]

It was against this background that volunteering began to be perceived in a new role: as a safe, constructive outlet for the otherwise unpredictable and destructive energies of disaffected young people. This view was strongly promoted by the media and the establishment, to the extent that it generated, in Dartington's phrase, a 'volunteer boom': 'The volunteer boom was viewed benignly from above. The Queen spoke in her 1965 Christmas message of "youth on the march". The *Daily Mirror* followed up with its 1966 crusade for youth in action. The Lord Mayor of London launched Venture '69 to acknowledge the work of young people in the community.'[8]

The involvement of young people in voluntary action was not without precedents. One thinks of, for example, the university settlements established in inner-city areas around the turn of the century; and the international youth movements which sprang up after each of the two world wars (such as, Service Civile Inter-nationale, International Voluntary Service, and Concordia). The key difference was that the earlier groups had tended to recruit, on the whole, middle-class and well-educated young people, and to harness their idealism in the service of those less well-off than themselves (whether it be in the East End of London or the ruined villages of northern France). The new sixties breed of organisations, on the other hand, saw volunteering more in terms of self-development for the less well-off, the less educated and the less able. In C. Allinson's phrase, volunteering underwent a transition 'from middle class altruism to an "industry" for the unsuccessful working class young'.[9]

Community Service Volunteers (CSV), founded by Alec Dickson in 1962, can perhaps be seen as the first of the major organisations in the 'young volunteer boom' mould. From the beginning, CSV prided itself on its policy of non-rejection, and its ability to find successful voluntary work placements for young people who would otherwise be written off as anti-social, 'difficult', or having nothing to offer (such as ex-Borstal trainees).

There followed a series of developments in a similar vein. The Newsom Report, in 1963, recommended that schoolchildren, particularly those of below-average academic ability, should be offered community service as part of a 'practical, realistic and (in the broadest sense) vocational' curriculum.[10] This was reinforced by the publication in 1968 of a Schools Council report on *Community Service and the Curriculum*.[11] In 1964 Anthony Steen set up Task Force, based on his experience of recruiting working-class teenagers in the East End of London to visit housebound pensioners. In 1968 he founded Young Volunteer Force Foundation (YVFF), intended as a national extension of the Task Force concept; the aim being 'to promote the role of the young volunteer by guiding his energy and enthusiasm into tackling urgent social problems'. In addition to the large and well-publicised organisations such as CSV, Task Force and YVFF, the mid to late 1960s saw the growth throughout the country of a large number of smaller, local groups with titles such as Young Volunteers, Youth Action, Student Community Action, and the like.

The End of Welfare Consensus

Towards the end of the 1960s, the assumptions and values about community service by young people which had underpinned the volunteer boom began to be questioned. This questioning reflected a shift in perception and attitude, not least on the part of those working in the voluntary sector itself. Within this, a number of inter-related factors can be identified:

- The voluntary sector had grown considerably in size and professionalism during the 1960s, and was beginning to feel confident enough to take a more 'political' stance (building on the experience of the many pressure groups and campaigning organisations which had enjoyed considerable growth in the preceding few years, such as Shelter and the Child Poverty Action Group).

- There was a general movement towards radical politics, particularly amongst younger people, growing out of the specific campaigns of the 1960s (Vietnam, civil rights, CND) into more fundamental critiques of the power structures in society (feminism, black power, neo-Marxism).
- There was a growing feeling that voluntary work was simply papering over the cracks of deprivation and the welfare state, whilst the real (i.e. political) problems were not being dealt with.
- Practitioners were becoming uneasy about the element of 'social control' implicit in the targeting of community service on young people. Also, whilst the young volunteer boom might have succeeded to some extent in getting rid of the middle-aged, middle-class stereotype of volunteering, it was in danger of simply replacing it with another stereotype.
- A credibility gap began to be perceived between what 'young volunteer' organisations promised and what they could deliver. They were supposed to be educating and socialising young people and, at the same time, providing effective personal services for people in need. In practice, the realism and wisdom of trying to combine both of these objectives was beginning to be questioned. There was a growing awareness that a more professional approach was needed, both to meeting the needs of the client or community, and to meeting the needs of the volunteer.

The publication of the Aves Report on *The Voluntary Worker in the Social Services* in 1969 represented something of a watershed in the development of volunteering.[12] After Aves, the volunteering movement might be said, in a sense, to have grown up. It began to distance itself from the 1960s identification with community service by young people, and to take a broader view of volunteering as a way in which people of all ages and backgrounds could be enabled to make a contribution to community services and activities. Following Seebohm,[13] Aves made a strong case for volunteer involvement as an integral part of social service provision, with volunteers complementing the services of professional staff. She linked this with the need for professional standards of good practice with regard to recruitment, training and support of volunteers. Apart from this, the Aves report was seminal in laying the foundations for the infrastructure of what may now be regarded as the volunteering movement: her recommendations led to the establishment of the Voluntary Services Unit in the Home Office, and of The Volunteer Centre; and the report provided much of the impetus for the development of a national network of volunteer bureaux, and the appointment of professional volunteer organisers in hundreds of statutory and voluntary agencies throughout the country.

One result of this change in direction in volunteering was that the various elements which had previously been held together, albeit under a degree of tension, within the young volunteer movement of the 1960s, began to crystallise and go their separate ways. In particular, there was tremendous growth in the field of community development, to the extent that the years 1968 to 1975 were labelled by Peter Baldock as a 'Community Work Boom'.[14] To some extent, this probably represented a reaction on the part of practitioners to the perceived shortcomings of the young volunteers/community service model. For instance, two of the archetypal sixties young volunteer agencies, Task Force and Young Volunteer Force Foundation, were both relaunched in the 1970s as community development agencies, following periods of considerable internal conflict. An unfortunate by-product of this process of fission in the early 1970s is the dichotomy which has existed ever since between volunteering and community work; with community workers, in particular, tending to regard volunteering as merely 'the soft end of community development'.[15]

In a similar fashion, the element of the young volunteer movement which was about the social and educational needs of young people began, in the early 1970s, to evolve a separate identity from the mainstream voluntary work field. The Youth Action movement, in the course of the 1970s, developed its own national infrastructure in the shape of the National Working Party of Young Volunteer Organisers and the Young Volunteer Resource Unit (YVRU), based at the National Youth Bureau. The YVRU played a leading role in the development of the concept of community involvement, which was basically about the application of community work principles of empowerment and self-determination to work with groups of young volunteers.[16]

At the same time, certain organisations, notably CSV, retained their commitment to the young volunteer/community service model; and the further evolution of this notion can be traced through such developments during the 1970s as Project Trident, the Youth Opportunities Programme, Community Industry and Community Service Orders. I shall be returning later in this chapter to the question of the relationship between volunteering and community service.

The next major change to have an impact on volunteering was the end of the postwar period of expansion in the welfare state, following the oil crisis and economic problems of the mid-1970s onwards. At the time the Aves Report was published, in 1969, the statutory services had been growing steadily for 20 years, and seemed set to continue growing indefinitely. Many services which had previously been provided by the voluntary sector had been taken over by the state. Aves expressed the generally held assumptions on which the resurgence in volunteering was based: that the welfare state would continue growing but that, within this, there was a continuing role for volunteers; and that this role should be increasingly integrated with, and complementary to, the statutory services.

The end of the era of growth in public spending heralded the end of the era of consensus about the welfare state. This had considerable implications for volunteering. In times of growth, it was generally accepted that volunteers had a legitimate role in providing additional services on the margins of the welfare state, and in pioneering new services. Once cutbacks became the order of the day, the fear was that volunteers would be sucked into the ever-widening gaps in core services.

One effect of this was to increase the suspicion with which paid staff, and trade unions, viewed volunteers. This, in turn, led to volunteer organisers, particular those in the National Health Service and social services, becoming more defensive. Considerable energy was devoted to the creation of policies, guidelines, and so on, which sought to allay the fears of paid staff by setting boundaries on volunteer involvement, and reasserting the 'complementary' principle. At a national level, The Volunteer Centre in 1975 issued *Guidelines for Relationships between Volunteers and Paid Non-Professional Workers* (the Drain Guidelines) which were based on consultations with the principal public sector unions.[17]

On the other hand, however, there was increasing interest by managers and politicians in how volunteers might help them square the circle of diminishing resources and increasing demand. In 1977 David Ennals, the Secretary of State for Social Services, launched the national Good Neighbour Campaign. A government working party on volunteers, set up by Prime Minister Callaghan and chaired by Stan Orme, MP, reported in March 1979, saying that: 'The use of volunteers should where possible be extended, especially in areas such as caring for the growing numbers of very elderly people, where the statutory services will have difficulty in meeting demand.'[18]

But most worrying of all to volunteer organisers trying to hold the

line for a complementary and harmonious relationship between paid
staff and volunteers, was to hear the Labour Social Services Secretary
– under considerable pressure from the Opposition and the media –
abandoning the Drain Guidelines, and giving health service managers
the go-ahead to use volunteers to maintain essential services during
the 1979 'Winter of Discontent'.

Volunteering in the 1980s

The promotion of volunteering by the Labour government of the late
1970s was essentially a pragmatic response to the problems in the
welfare state caused by the country's economic and industrial
difficulties. In contrast, the Conservative government, which came to
power in 1979, embraced this approach with ideological zeal. This
can be seen in the alacrity with which the new administration
capitalised on the precedent set by David Ennals in the 'Winter of
Discontent'. In November 1979, it issued a new NHS Circular which
effectively threw the Drain Guidelines out of the window, and
encouraged NHS managers to take immediate steps to recruit
volunteers to be deployed in any future emergency.[19]

Support for volunteering and the voluntary sector had already
been identified as a plank of Tory policy before the election:
Conservative Central Office had published a pamphlet on the subject
in 1978;[20] Patrick Jenkin, then Shadow Social Services Secretary,
made a series of speeches during 1978 in which he praised the virtues
of 'the voluntary movement', and contrasted them with the vices of
'the socialist state'; and a paragraph was included in the Conservative
election manifesto promising encouragement for 'the voluntary
movement and self-help groups working in partnership with the
statutory services'.

The burden of the Conservative rhetoric was that the statutory
services were bureaucratic, inefficient, socialistic, and left no room
for individual responsibility; whereas the voluntary movement was
cost-effective, independent, flexible, and encouraged self-help and
individual responsibility. Previous assumptions that volunteers
should complement or supplement statutory provision were turned
on their head; instead, it was suggested that it was the role of the
statutory services to supplement the voluntary movement. Margaret
Thatcher, speaking at the Annual Conference of the Women's Royal
Voluntary Service in January 1981, summed up this approach:

However rich Britain becomes . . . there's no way and no budget
that could produce statutory services to meet the needs which as
volunteers you now satisfy . . . I believe that the volunteer
movement is at the heart of all our social welfare provision; that
the statutory services are the supportive ones, underpinning
where necessary, filling the gaps and helping the helpers . . . The
willingness of men and women to give service is one of freedom's
greatest safeguards. It ensures that caring remains free from
political control. It leaves men and women independent enough
to meet needs as they see them, and not only as the state
provides.[21]

When Mrs Thatcher speaks here of the volunteer movement, it
should be noted that she does not necessarily mean volunteer, as
such. In this and similar statements by Conservative politicians,
phrases such as 'the volunteer movement' are used fairly loosely, as
an umbrella term embracing not only volunteering, but also the
voluntary sector, self-help groups, and the informal sector (i.e.
family, friends and neighbours). The term 'voluntarism' has been
widely used to describe this fusion of different, though related
concepts.

The Conservative campaign on behalf of voluntarism was not,
however, universally welcomed by those in the voluntarism field. For
example, the Association of Community Workers published a paper
in 1982 arguing that:

Voluntarism has re-surfaced in the politics of welfare in the
1980s. Primarily this results from the Government's promotion
of voluntarism as a central part of its social policies, alongside its
determination to implement unprecedented cuts in public
spending. Both are linked directly to current economic policies
and the rapid increase in unemployment . . . Voluntarism is a
soft, beguiling message. The cuts and unemployment are real
and brutal. Together they represent insidious attempts to deny
and dismantle essential tenets on which the welfare state
stands.[22]

Nor was the debate about voluntarism a simple case of right versus
left. It was not just the anti-welfare right calling for a shift away from
the traditional statist approach to service provision. Influential
critiques of the welfare state were also coming from a variety of other
perspectives: for example, Beresford and Croft calling for community

control of social services; Hadley and Hatch, and Gladstone, advocating a more pluralistic mixed economy of welfare; the Barclay Report arguing the case for community social work; and the polemics of Ivan Illich on the disabling effect of professions and institutions.[23]

This indicates the essential ambiguity of the voluntarism debate: the same rhetoric may conceal diametrically opposite points of view. Consider, for example, the following statement:

We recognise that voluntary organisations can often provide a better and more sensitive pattern of service than a local authority can. They can often respond much more quickly to need and be more innovative ... Similarly, voluntary groups can generally work more cost-effectively than large bureaucracies and are more likely to involve the local community.

This could easily have come from a speech by Margaret Thatcher or Patrick Jenkin of the early 1980s. In fact, it was part of the preface to the Labour Greater London Council's 1982 guide to grant aid for voluntary organisations and community groups, written by Ken Livingstone.[24] It was the Labour GLC's policy of greatly increased support for the voluntary sector – embracing, as it did, a wide range of groups promoting the rights of minority communities – that formed a major plank of the government and media campaign leading to the abolition of the GLC. Patrick Jenkin's promise that 'worthwhile' voluntary effort would have nothing to fear from the abolition represented a significant qualification to the Conservative Party's apparent role as the champion of voluntarism.

Whilst the political debate about voluntarism continued, another issue rose to the top of the social policy agenda in the first half of the 1980s with the massive increase in unemployment. Once again, politicians and the public turned to voluntary work for solutions to a pressing social problem.

People's fears about the social consequences of mass unemployment were given substance in the summer of 1981, when riots took place in London, Bristol and Liverpool. Shortly after the riots, and in response to them, the Prime Minister announced that the government would be bringing forward proposals to encourage unemployed people to do voluntary work. This led to the introduction, in 1982, of two separate programmes: Opportunities for Volunteering (OFV), run by the Department of Health and Social Security (DHSS); and Voluntary Projects Programme (VPP), run by the Manpower Services Commission (MSC). The logic was fairly obvious: since the devil finds work for idle hands to do, why not keep the unemployed constructively (if not gainfully) occupied with voluntary work? Allied to this, was the proposition that there were all these people sitting around on the dole doing nothing, and there were all these tasks needing to be done in the community which society cannot afford to pay for, so why not put the two together? Thus the unemployed would be able to brush up their work skills, and the community would get some useful work done. There is perhaps a parallel here with what happened in the 1960s. Then, society felt threatened by the younger generation. Now, it felt threatened by the unemployed. In both cases, voluntary work was seen as a convenient safety-valve to help control the deviant group.

The immediate result of these government initiatives, as far as those involved in the organisation of volunteers were concerned, was confusion and anxiety about this sudden switch in their perceived role. In March 1982, The Volunteer Centre and the National Council for Voluntary Organisations (NCVO) protested to the government about the voluntary sector being used as a 'dumping ground for some of the most intractable problems of the labour market'. They complained about the confusion arising from the lack of co-ordination between different government departments, and about the unrealistic expectations being generated (the Chancellor in his budget speech had spoken of 100,000 places being created on VPP alone). 'We have no idea what we are supposed to be doing', said Peter Stubbings, Deputy Director of The Volunteer Centre.[25]

However, following the initial confusion and uncertainty, the voluntary sector was quick to adapt to the changing social policy agenda, and the new opportunities this brought. The DHSS had no problem in putting together a consortium of 15 voluntary organisations to administer the OFV fund, and the £1 million allocated to the General Fund in May 1982 was all spent by November, with another £5 million of bids still outstanding. Colin Ball summed this up in a 1985 paper for The Volunteer Centre:

People scoffed when the idea of voluntary work by the unemployed was first mooted by the Chancellor, but when the programmes came along not only did [the voluntary organisations] rush in to collect the cash but, goodness, they set up a consortium as well to dole out the 'Opps' cash on behalf of the Government, much of it to themselves, naturally.[26]

As a result of the new schemes linking unemployment with

volunteering, practitioners found themselves grappling with the fundamental question of the relationship between voluntary work and paid work. Voluntary sector involvement in job-creation and training schemes from the mid-1970s onwards had already tended to create a certain blurring of the boundaries, as the various MSC schemes generally involved an element of community service, which in many respects resembled volunteering. This tendency, however, was greatly increased after 1980, due to the massive growth in MSC programmes, coupled with the steady erosion of rates of pay on job-creation schemes, as the principle of 'the rate for the job' was replaced by that of 'benefit plus'. The confusion was compounded by the introduction of OFV and VPP, alongside the job-creation and training schemes, specifically recruiting the unemployed as volunteers. In the light of this, people began to question whether there was any point in seeking to maintain a distinction between paid work and volunteering. Yet this distinction – and the notion of volunteers and paid workers having different but complementary roles – had underpinned policy and practice in volunteering since Aves. If this principle was abandoned, what would replace it?

One response to this was to seek to redefine volunteering so as to accommodate the blurring of boundaries which was taking place. A number of statements issued by The Volunteer Centre took this approach. In its 1983 *Charter for Volunteers*, the Centre defined volunteering as 'work undertaken on behalf of self or others outside the immediate family, not *directly* in return for wages, undertaken by free choice, not required by the state or its agencies' (emphasis mine).[27] The use of the word 'directly' here is clearly intended to leave the door open for some kinds of paid work to be defined as volunteering. In *Policies towards Unemployment and Volunteering*, also issued in 1983, The Volunteer Centre made the point more explicitly:

> The definition of volunteering must embrace a great variety of work outside the labour market, including such diverse activities as paid street warden schemes, volunteer-like work within the programmes of the Manpower Services Commission that offer allowances or marginal wages, community exchanges where work is bartered, and self-help groups.[28]

The reasoning behind this is spelt out in Mark Rankin's 1985 paper, *Working in the Margin*:

The response of the Government to the growing imbalance between the labour market and the labour force has been to broaden the margin at the edge of the traditional labour market, and to encourage the growth of all types of activities by some of the 3.27 million registered unemployed people in the hope that marginal work can form a bridge back into the labour market. Voluntary work by unemployed people is just one aspect of these marginal activities.[29]

There were perhaps both pragmatic and principled reasons for this redefinition of volunteering. In pragmatic terms, it legitimised the process whereby many voluntary agencies were increasingly acting as delivery agents for government 'special employment measures'. On a more principled level, there was the feeling that upholding philo-sophical distinctions between voluntary work and paid work was a luxury which could no longer be afforded, given the need to respond to the urgent and brutal reality of unemployment. Beyond this, there was also a view that maybe the current unemployment crisis was merely a prelude to a post-industrial society in which many of the traditional distinctions between paid and unpaid work would become irrelevant.[30]

There are, however, a number of objections to redefining volunteering in this way. One obvious difficulty is that most people equate volunteering with being unpaid, and therefore to seek to define it differently could be seen as perverse and potentially confusing. Secondly, as Titmuss pointed out in *The Gift Relationship*, there is an important psychological difference between that which is given and that which is sold, and this applies to work at least as much as anything else.[31] Thirdly, putting volunteering in the same market-place as paid work is likely to result in a further erosion of wage levels, particularly for those already in the lowest-paid and most marginal jobs. And fourthly, it is just not realistic to see voluntary work as a substitute for paid work, or volunteering as a solution to unemployment.

This last point was reinforced by the various evaluative studies of schemes linking unemployment with volunteering which appeared around the mid-1980s, including Gay and Hatch on VPP, Doyle and Mocroft on OFV, and Ford on the role of volunteer bureaux.[32] The general conclusion was that while voluntary work could be of great value for a minority of unemployed people, it was largely irrelevant to the majority. It was perhaps partly this realisation which led to much of the steam going out of the 'unemployment and volunteering' debate after around 1987/88. Another factor was that, following the initial turmoil, the various special programmes had been gradually absorbed into the mainstream of volunteering activity. The Voluntary Projects Programme (VPP), having first been merged into the Community Programme/Employment Training, was subsequently relaunched as Community Opportunities, a scheme run by some volunteer bureaux to help 'graduates' of ET to find voluntary work. And OFV has continued, on the whole, to be used to support general volunteer projects in the health and social services field, often with little or no real attempt to target volunteer recruitment on the unemployed. Perhaps the most significant factor, however, is that from around 1988 onwards, with the unemployment figures starting to fall, and other problems beginning to assert themselves (inflation, interest rates, poll tax, and so on), concerns about unemployment began to fade from the government and public consciousness.

Volunteering in the 1990s

What issues of social policy are dominating discussion in the volunteering field as we move into the 1990s? One key issue is certainly that of community care. Community care – enabling people to live independent lives in the community rather than looking after them in hospitals or institutions – has been the theoretical goal of government policy since the 1950s. It is only since the end of the 1970s, however, that it has been put into practice with real vigour.

There is clearly considerable potential for volunteers to assist in the transition from institutional to community care, and to provide continuing support for people within the community. In the field, much good and innovative practice has been developed around this theme over the last 10 years or so; including advocacy schemes, independent living schemes, hospital aftercare projects, befriending schemes, 'pop-in' projects, and many others.

The government, however, appears to have blown hot and cold on the volunteer contribution to community care. The strident rhetoric on voluntarism of the early years of the Thatcher government seemed to suggest that volunteers would practically take over the delivery of social services. Even if desirable, this was clearly never a realistic goal. Eventually, rhetoric had to give way to reality; and when – following Sir Roy Griffiths' review of community care services – the White Paper *Caring for People* finally emerged in 1989, it contained virtually no mention of volunteers. It did, however, lay great stress on the role of the voluntary sector in taking over the services currently provided by social services departments, as local authorities shift from the role of service provider to that of enabler.[33]

So it seems that the government, having initially overplayed the role of volunteers in community care, is now underplaying it. This could have unfortunate consequences for both volunteering and community care. Much of the voluntary work currently taking place in the community care field – including some of the best and most innovative practice – is being done by volunteers working under the auspices of the statutory health and social services. Following the National Health Service and Community Care Act, which became law in June 1990, social services departments and district health authorities will increasingly divest themselves of their service-provision role, and therefore will begin to withdraw from their role as 'employers' of volunteers. In consequence, much of this good, innovative work will be put at risk.

Will there be a corresponding expansion of volunteering in the private companies, non-profit organisations and 'opted-out' health service trusts which will be picking up the contracts to provide the former district health authority and social services department services? As far as the private companies are concerned, there is little reason to think that they will regard the development of volunteering as a high priority, particularly if they realise that volunteer support costs will reduce their profit margins. As for voluntary organisations and opted-out hospitals, many of them clearly do have a track record in involving volunteers, but the question is to what extent this will continue to be a priority as they are drawn into the contract culture. The danger is that in a climate dominated by cost accounting, penalty clauses and output measures, the resources required to underpin volunteer involvement – organisers' salaries and volunteers' expenses – will be seen as an unnecessary frill. Indeed, one possible consequence of the contract culture is that it may lead to the replacement of volunteers by paid staff in certain voluntary sector-run services. Particularly in large-scale, labour-intensive services – such as day centres and meals on wheels – voluntary sector managers, faced with tightly drawn contracts and service specifications, may opt for the relative stability and control of employing paid workers rather than continuing to rely on the vagaries of volunteer supply and goodwill.

Fears have also been expressed as to the effects of the contract culture on those areas of volunteer activity which are not directly concerned with service provision. The White Paper acknowledged that activities such as advocacy, campaigning and pressure-group work are valid roles for voluntary organisations, and require financial support through grant aid rather than contracts. But it remains to be seen what priority these areas will get when it comes to competing for the limited cash available for community care. At the same time, there is a danger that fears about the effects of privatisation, opting-out and contracting-out upon staff pay and conditions of employment will prompt unions to take a more negative stance on volunteer involvement, thus further compromising the ability of volunteers to play a full role in the development of community care.

There is, therefore, a worrying prospect that government policy, far from placing volunteers 'at the heart of all our social welfare provision', may have the effect of starving volunteering of resources and squeezing volunteers out of community care.

Active Citizenship

The other issue which is generating much debate within the volunteering field as we enter the 1990s is that of citizenship, together with its more dynamic relative – active citizenship. According to the *Guardian*, the active citizen first appeared in February 1988 in a speech by the then Home Secretary, Douglas Hurd. The *Guardian* suggests that active citizenship was a concept invented by the wet end of the Conservative Party (though subsequently taken up by Margaret Thatcher and John MacGregor, among others), to help reconcile the apparent harsh materialism of Thatcherism with the more caring values of traditional one-nation Toryism. 'Mr Hurd's intent', said the *Guardian*, 'was to commit his party to a broader, nobler vision than the restless pursuit of material success which some had come to believe it was now all about.'[34] The active citizen therefore clearly had a good deal in common with the middle-class, philanthropic volunteer of the nineteenth century. He or she was someone who combined success with caring, who was willing to put something back into society – through giving money to voluntary organisations or, better still, direct and personal effort – in order to help those who were not so successful. Equally important, he or she was not a 'moaning Minnie': the active citizen would not sit back and declare that the government ought to spend more money on a particular problem, but would roll up his or her sleeves and do something about it.

A slightly different view of the active citizen was given by John Patten, MP, in a speech in June 1989. In this, he made it clear that he more or less equated active citizenship with volunteering, making the point that 'anyone can be an active citizen'. He went on to say that 'it is a form of behaviour which we are seeking to encourage'; and, by way of illustration, he detailed the various ways in which the government was supporting volunteering and the voluntary sector.[35] This is very much in tune with government policy, as stated in the *Efficiency Scrutiny of Government Funding of the Voluntary Sector*, which recommends that priority be given to funding organisations 'which promote the recruitment and use of volunteers', on the grounds that volunteering 'is a desirable activity in its own right, and . . . a very cost-effective way of providing desirable services'.[36]

Thus on one level, the active citizenship debate may be viewed as merely an extension of the Conservative government's promotion of voluntarism. Meanwhile, however, the notion of citizenship has also been taken up by a number of influential individuals since 1988 and, at the time of writing, various proposals are emerging which could have major implications for volunteering. In particular, 1990 saw both the publication of the report of the Speaker's Commission on Citizenship,[37] and the launch of the Prince of Wales' 'Volunteers' scheme.

The Commission on Citizenship was established in 1988, under the auspices of the Speaker of the House of Commons, following an initial approach by Elisabeth Hoodless, Director of Community Service Volunteers (CSV), to Frances Morrell, former Leader of the Inner London Education Authority. Ms Hoodless wanted to know why schools, in general, seemed to be doing so little about citizenship.

Given this origin, it is not surprising that whilst the Commission's report devotes some space to a review of the political, legal, social and civil rights associated with citizenship, its main focus is on the relationship between citizenship, education and volunteering. The Commission recommends that citizenship studies should be systematically taught in schools, and recognised as a theme within the National Curriculum. It also argues for a general expansion of volunteering on a national level, to be achieved by a greater promotion of opportunities, on the one hand, and by the introduction of a formal system of rewards and incentives on the other. The Commission's view is that citizenship activities should start with the study of citizenship principles in school; but that this theoretical work should be complemented by the experience of practical community service. This is where the Prince of Wales' 'Volunteers' scheme fits in. It was developed by the Prince's Trust in collaboration with the Commission on Citizenship, and is seen as a vehicle for delivering the many thousands of community service opportunities for young people which the Commission believes to be necessary (the eventual aim is to take on 100,000 young people per year).

In considering the implications of these initiatives for the future of volunteering, it is worth looking somewhat further back than 1988 for their antecedents. In doing so, we can throw light on the underlying themes – the 'hidden agenda' – of the current debate.

The way in which, following the Aves Report, the concepts of volunteering and community service began to diverge was touched on earlier in this chapter. In many ways, the current proposals on citizenship seem to hark back to the pre-Aves young volunteer ethos. The report of the Speaker's Commission on Citizenship seems to fit comfortably within the tradition of the Newsom Report, the Bessey Report, and the Schools Council Working Party, in seeking to place community service within the education and youth service curriculum. The Prince's Trust scheme, on the other hand, seems to follow in the footsteps of the classic sixties young volunteering organisations, such as CSV, Task Force and YVFF. It is notable, also, that the personal vision of Dr Alec Dickson and Elisabeth Hoodless, founder and director respectively of CSV, has been a major influence in the continuing development of the community service movement, up to and including the Commission on Citizenship and the Prince's Trust 'Volunteer' scheme.

Community service, after its separation from the volunteering movement at the start of the 1970s, developed in a variety of ways. It was part of Project Trident (initiated by IBM in 1971), and the Outward Bound City Challenge programme. In 1973 the Home Office introduced Community Service Orders as a punitive/ rehabilitative sentencing option for adult offenders. Also, the 1970s saw the growth of a plethora of training and job-creation schemes for the unemployed, all involving an element of community service: including Community Industry, Youth Opportunities Programme, Special Temporary Employment Programme, Job Creation Programme and Community Programme.

It was against this background that, towards the end of the 1970s, a group of individuals got together to promote the concept of a national community service scheme for young people. Prominent members of this group, which called itself the Commission on Youth and the Needs of the Nation, were Dr Alec Dickson, Elisabeth Hoodless and Nicholas Stacey (then Director of Kent Social Services). The group's report, published in 1980, argued that there was a vast amount of unmet need in the community, which could and should be met by the mobilisation of large numbers of young people in community service.[38] This was backed up by a report commissioned from a researcher at the London School of Economics, which aimed to demonstrate the viability of such a scheme for Nationwide Social Service.[39]

The Commission on Youth and the Needs of the Nation evolved into Youth Call, which published a discussion document in 1981 subtitled *A Debate on Youth and Service to the Community*. This argued that a scheme of national community service was attractive for the following reasons:

> Philosophically, because it would appeal to young people's idealism and give them an opportunity to serve and help revivify the Social Services. Politically, because if it were taken up by large numbers of young people it could markedly reduce unemployment. Economically, because the net cost would be significantly less than not utilising their energies.[40]

Youth Call attracted national press coverage, and excited a certain amount of public interest. The Social Democratic Party was even moved to get in on the act by publishing a proposal of its own under the title of *Count Us In*.[41] In the end, however, the mooted national community service scheme did not materialise. There was unease, in the volunteering movement and elsewhere, about its implications as regards cheap labour, job substitution, and the massaging of the unemployment figures. The question of compulsion was perhaps of even greater concern. Without an element of this, the scheme would clearly not have been viable on the scale envisaged by its proponents, but many people felt uncomfortable about proposals which had connotations of forced labour, despite the arguments of Youth Call that such a scheme would in fact be more egalitarian.

Youth Call themselves recognised this problem, and referred to it in their discussion paper:

> One possible way out of the impasse between voluntary and obligatory is to reward those who volunteer. This could be done by encouraging employers to give preference to those who have done such service. Differential awards could also be made, whether they be student grants or unemployment benefits. Perhaps it could become like Jury Service, a normal requirement from which it is possible to be exempted.[42]

Nine years on, members of the Commission on Citizenship have clearly taken on board the lessons of Youth Call, hoping that the replacement of the element of compulsion by a system of rewards and incentives will make the latest proposals more acceptable. Thus, they suggest that citizenship activities should be included in academic records of achievement, and in the criteria for selection to further and higher education; that employers should recognise volunteering in their recruitment and promotion policies; and that certificates, medals and public honours should be awarded on a systematic basis for voluntary service. Elisabeth Hoodless, in September 1990, went further than this, proposing that the government should introduce a 'loan forgiveness' scheme under which students completing a period of voluntary service would have their student loans written off.[43]

Values of Volunteering

A theme of this chapter has been the way in which volunteering has grown up since the 1960s. It has acquired an infrastructure of its own, and it has developed a set of values. In 1989 The Volunteer Centre UK set out to summarise what it felt to be the main values of volunteering, in a leaflet entitled *The Promotion of Volunteering*. This lists seven key 'propositions' which it argues should underpin policy and practice on volunteering. The first of these is: 'We believe that people who do voluntary work should do so out of personal choice, not because they have been coerced by laws, taxation or any other institutional regulation. We recognise that there are many ways of "encouraging" people to do "voluntary" work that contravene this principle of free choice.'[44] The paper goes on to argue that if volunteering is about the freedom to choose to participate, the corollary of this is 'the freedom to choose to remain passive if we so wish'. It condemns attempts to persuade people to volunteer which 'lean heavily on moral blackmail'. In contrast with this, within the concept of community service (and within its current manifestation, active citizenship), there is an implicit sense of moral obligation – even of restitution, or atonement. For example, Community Service Orders, and the proposed student loan forgiveness scheme, are particularly clear embodiments of the notion of community service as paying off a debt to society. This is fundamentally in conflict with the principle, enunciated by The Volunteer Centre UK, of volunteering as a freely chosen activity.

The Political Dimension of Volunteering

Clearly, as we enter the 1990s, there is something of a struggle going on for the soul of volunteering. And this struggle is essentially a political one. Although the Speaker's Commission on Citizenship and the Prince's Trust are non-partisan bodies in political terms, their ideas about volunteering are much in tune with current government thinking. The taking up of the theme of active citizenship by various prominent Conservative politicians has already been mentioned. It is interesting, too, to note that Elisabeth Hoodless's student loan forgiveness proposal, according to the *Observer*, originated at a confidential Downing Street seminar chaired by Brian Griffiths, Mrs Thatcher's chief policy adviser.[45] In this context, it is perhaps also worth noting the proposals made in September 1990 by the No Turning Back group of Conservative MPs, intended for inclusion in the Conservative election manifesto. Central to these was the proposal to privatise the national insurance and social security system, and that 'young people with no means of paying into the system could be required to do community work as an alternative form of contribution'.[46] Taking these things together, the implication would appear to be that, particularly in the event of a Conservative victory at the next election, there will be increased pressure on volunteering to participate in moves towards national community service and workfare-type 'work for benefit' schemes.

Meanwhile, on the other side of the political divide, there are signs that the Labour Party has begun to reassess its attitude towards volunteering. In the face of the Conservatives'. advocacy of voluntarism, Labour's stance on volunteering through the 1980s was generally rather ambivalent and defensive. At the time of writing, however, Labour is seeking through its Policy Review to re-establish its credentials in terms of support for voluntary activity. David Blunkett, MP, gave an indication of this at his Aves Lecture at The Volunteer Centre UK annual general meeting in 1988, when he declared that 'in all areas of politics there needs to be a commitment to volunteering and voluntary organisations'.[47]

Labour also set up a working party, chaired by Alf Dubbs, to consider its policy on the voluntary sector/and volunteering, and, at the time of writing, a consultation paper is under discussion. Indications are that Labour will acknowledge the trend towards greater pluralism in service delivery, with an increasing role for voluntary organisations and volunteers. At the same time, it will re-emphasise the importance of co-operative and community development approaches and the need to give priority to minority groups. Labour policy, in contrast with Conservative, is also likely to stress the need to ensure that volunteers do not threaten the interests of paid staff; perhaps in terms of a return to the principles of the Drain Guidelines.

The outcome of the general election in 1991 or 1992 will, therefore, clearly be important in influencing the future direction and development of volunteering in this country. Perhaps this is to be regretted, if as The Volunteer Centre UK says, 'for genuine volunteering to survive, it must be kept apart from politics'.[48] On the other hand, it is a sign of the polarised and politicised times in which we live; and perhaps, too, it is a sign of the increasingly central role which voluntary activity plays in these times.

Conclusion

This chapter has sought to show how, over the last three decades, perceptions and expectations of volunteering have been conditioned by the major social problems and concerns of the time. In the 1960s, volunteering was seen as an antidote to, or palliative for, anti-social behaviour by teenagers. In the 1970s and 1980s, it was expected to help make up for reductions in public expenditure, to curb trade union power, and to alleviate unemployment. Currently, the talk is of volunteering as a way of promoting better citizenship. It will be interesting to see what roles society devises for volunteering in the 1990s.

CHAPTER 2

AN UNEASY ALLIANCE: VOLUNTEERS AND TRADE UNIONS

Justin Davis Smith

Introduction

The history of relations between volunteers and organised labour is an uneasy one. The British Labour movement, steeped in a collectivist philosophy, has opposed volunteers as a throwback to nineteenth-century charity and dependency and, especially during periods of economic stagnation, as a threat to paid jobs. However, it is the use by successive governments this century of members of the general public to break strikes, most notably during the General Strike of 1926, which has done more than anything else to increase trade union mistrust of volunteers. This chapter examines the uneasy relationship between volunteers and trade unions since the Second World War, with particular reference to the role of volunteers during strikes. It concludes that tensions have eased in recent years and predicts an improvement in relations in the next decade and beyond.

An Uneasy Alliance

During the immediate postwar years, with sustained growth in the economy and relatively high levels of public expenditure, the conflict between volunteers and the Labour movement remained latent. The postwar settlement which ushered in the welfare state and witnessed the rapid extension of public ownership, relegated voluntary action in society very much to a secondary role. Prior to the 1960s there were very few volunteers within the statutory sector to fan the flames of discord. In 1967, for example, there were only 14 voluntary service co-ordinators in the whole of the National Health Service. The situation began to change in the late 1960s and 1970s as successive balance of payments crises and cuts in public expenditure, coupled with mounting criticism of the bureaucracy and lack of accountability of the public services, led to a massive expansion of grass-roots voluntary organisations and of the use of volunteers in the statutory sector.

The publication of two reports at this time – the Seebohm Report and the Aves Report,[1] both of which called for an expansion of voluntary effort in the health and personal social services, gave impetus to this trend. By 1973 there were over 200 hospital volunteer co-ordinators in place, responsible for the recruitment and deployment of many thousands of volunteers. Under this pressure, the uneasy postwar alliance between volunteers and paid workers began to break down.

Symptomatic of this climate of mistrust was the passage of a resolution in the early 1970s by the health service union, the Confederation of Health Service Employees (COHSE), seeking to ban all volunteers from hospitals. The situation was exacerbated by the participation of volunteers in the health service disputes of 1973. In November in County Durham, for example, 400 volunteers were deployed by the county council to maintain emergency services during a strike of ambulance drivers. This was despite a plea from the director of the newly formed Volunteer Centre that the government should call in the army to staff the emergency services rather than risk threatening the long-term placement of volunteers. In this period of increasing tension, The Volunteer Centre took the initiative in bringing together representatives of the public sector unions and volunteer-involving organisations in the health and personal social services, to thrash out an agreement on the use of volunteer labour. The Drain Guidelines – so-called after Mr Geoffrey Drain, the chair of the working party and general secretary of the National and Local Government Officers' Association (NALGO) – addressed many of the contentious issues raised by the deployment of volunteers, including job substitution and the role of volunteers during industrial disputes. The Guidelines were unequivocal in their condemnation of the use of volunteers to undermine trade union bargaining power. Guideline no.7 laid down that 'volunteers in the situation of industrial action should undertake no more voluntary work than they would do in the normal situation', while Guideline no.8 advised volunteers not to cross picket lines in the event of trade union non-cooperation.[2]

The Drain Guidelines were a valiant attempt to reconcile the conflicting interests of volunteers and the paid workforce. They sought to allay the genuine fears of the union movement that volunteers, especially in a period of economic stagnation, posed a threat to paid jobs while, at the same time, giving full recognition to the rights of the volunteer and to the valuable role of voluntary action in society. The importance of the document lay in the tripartite structure of the working group from which it arose. Even COHSE, which only a few years previously had voted to oppose any co-operation with volunteers, felt able to put its name to an agreement which spoke of 'the value of voluntary activity' to society.

The Guidelines held up well prior to the industrial troubles of the Labour administration in 1978/79. During the so-called Winter of Discontent, volunteers found themselves in the front-line of the industrial unrest in the health and public services and increasingly in conflict with the trade union movement.

At the outset of the disputes, David Ennals, the Secretary of State for Social Services, called on hospital authorities to work within the framework of the Guidelines and to consult with the unions before calling in volunteers. He told Parliament that he was anxious 'to avoid conflict with the trade unions that would jeopardise the long term usefulness of volunteers'.[3] As the stoppages spread, so the pressure increased on the government to take more concerted action. At the beginning of February, the leader of the Opposition, Margaret Thatcher, made a public call for the deployment of volunteers. Speaking at the Conference of the National Young Conservatives in Bournemouth, she said: 'We have a great national tradition of voluntary service. There are enough people in this country resolved to keep it going, and determined not to yield to bullying. At such a time it would be the duty of the government to harness this spirited reserve to the service of our people.'[4]

On 15 March 1979, Ennals informed Parliament that he had authorised the health authorities to call for volunteers to maintain essential services. The reaction from the unions was predictably fierce. The general secretary of COHSE, Albert Spanswick, accused the government of strike-breaking and of putting at risk relations between volunteers and paid workers. The press made much of reports of trade union hostility and picket-line violence towards volunteers.

The true extent of volunteer involvement in the strikes and the nature of relations between volunteers and the unions can be gauged from an unpublished report compiled at the time by The Volunteer Centre.[5] The report contradicts the commonly held view that vast numbers of volunteers were deployed during the dispute, and that hostility between volunteers and trade unions was widespread.

The report was compiled in the Autumn of 1979 from a questionnaire distribute 1 to all voluntary service co-ordinators in the health service. The report analysed volunteer activity in hospitals where a trade union code of conduct to maintain essential services was being operated, as well as in hospitals where no emergency cover was provided. Of the 114 hospitals in the survey where the code of conduct was recognised only 10 per cent reported an increase in the use of regular volunteers during the strike. In 75 per cent of hospitals, volunteer levels remained unchanged and in 12 per cent all volunteers were withdrawn. The figures were only slightly different in hospitals where emergency cover was withheld by the unions. Here 51 per cent reported no change in the levels of regular volunteer activity, 27 per cent reported an increase, while volunteers were withdrawn in 19 per cent of hospitals where the code of conduct was not in operation.

Most regular volunteers did not increase their workloads during the strike. Neither did the majority of health authorities make a call for additional voluntary assistance. The Volunteer Centre report shows that only 15 per cent of health authorities recruited additional labour, although 30 per cent did so where emergency cover was not provided. These findings, which suggest that trade union claims of volunteer strike-breaking were overstated, are confirmed by evidence given in the House of Commons on 3 April. This revealed that voluntary helpers were being utilised in only 32 of the 199 health authorities in England and in only 8 of the 45 ambulance authorities.

The government's advice to health authorities on 14 March to call for volunteers to maintain essential services, seems to have had little impact on the situation. The Volunteer Centre report reveals that of 125 voluntary service co-ordinators who replied to the questionnaire there were only six cases where local managers took action to recruit additional volunteers as a direct consequence of Ennals' intervention.

The findings on trade union reaction to volunteer involvement during the strikes are equally illuminating. In those settings where the trade union code of conduct was recognised, the attitude of local unions to the activity of regular volunteers was found to be 48 per cent formal endorsement, 38 per cent passive support, and only 2 per cent hostility. Where union cover for emergency services was not provided, hostility towards volunteers was slightly greater, but was still only 3 per cent. In over 50 per cent of hospitals not covered by the code of conduct, a formal agreement was reached between unions and management over volunteer levels, and in a further 29 per cent of cases union acquiescence was secured. Not surprisingly, given memories of 1926, union hostility was greatest where outside volunteers were recruited to replace the strikers. Yet, even in these most provocative of situations, formal agreement was reached between the unions and management in over 30 per cent of cases.

The Drain Guidelines stood up remarkably well to the industrial troubles of 1979. The Volunteer Centre report showed that where the code of conduct was in place, 80 per cent of voluntary service co-ordinators felt that the Guidelines were helpful, and over 50 per cent expressed satisfaction where the code was not recognised. Nevertheless, there was opposition from some quarters. One senior Conservative MP wrote to The Volunteer Centre stating his view that the Guidelines were 'deplorable', and seemed 'more concerned with buttressing union power than with helping those who are the unfortunate victims of industrial action'.

The Thatcher Years

The return to office of a Conservative administration in 1979, pledged to curbing trade union power and to rolling back the frontiers of the state, was to have a profound impact on relations between volunteers and organised labour. Tory thinking on a new code to cover relations between volunteers and unions was outlined during the election campaign by the spokesman on health and social services, Patrick Jenkin. In a speech on 15 April he said:

The carefully drawn 'volunteer code' covering the role of volunteers in industrial disputes proved almost unworkable during the recent disputes in the NHS. If one really believes that 'patients come first', then it simply will not do to let patients suffer for fear of upsetting trade unions on strike.[6]

Action followed quickly after the general election. In November, Jenkin, as Secretary of State for Health and Social Services in the new Thatcher administration, issued a circular to hospital authorities on emergency planning in the event of future industrial unrest in the health service.[7] The circular cut right across the carefully negotiated

Drain Guidelines which had called for union co-operation in the deployment of volunteers.

'It is clear', the circular stated, 'that, properly organised, volunteers can make a valuable contribution to the maintenance of services to patients'. For that reason, health authorities 'should, if they feel it necessary during a dispute, make such use of volunteers as they think fit'. Consideration should also be given to how health authorities 'can tap the help the general public are usually and spontaneously prepared to offer in response to the needs of sick people'. Ministerial support was offered to any authority which chose to make use of volunteers during industrial unrest. Emergency preparations, the circular stressed, were to start immediately and were not to wait until a dispute had begun.

This circular in effect offered health authorities a blank cheque to take whatever action they deemed necessary to break a strike in the health service. It was seen by the trade union movement as a strike-breakers' charter. The Opposition called for its immediate withdrawal and warned that its presence would seriously undermine good-will between volunteers and paid staff. Stan Orme, the Shadow Social Services Secretary, said 'if Mrs Thatcher puts the flag up and marches in front of volunteers, then we will certainly oppose her because she will do countless damage for the future'.[8]

In the summer of 1980 the Conservative government turned its attention once more to the question of the use of civilian volunteers in industrial disputes. In June the Prime Minister, in answer to a parliamentary question on whether any proposals were in hand to encourage the use of volunteers to replace striking workers in the public services, said that she 'recognised the value of the work of the established voluntary organisations in helping to maintain essential public services in an emergency'. Mrs Thatcher also had 'no doubt about the willingness of private individuals voluntarily to help in such situations, where they can usefully do so'. In July the press reported on secret negotiations taking place within the Civil Contingencies Unit of the Cabinet on the use of volunteers during strikes.[9] To place these discussions in context it is necessary to look briefly at the history of emergency planning in this country.

Volunteers as Strike-Breakers

Civilian volunteers have been seen by successive governments this century as an integral part of emergency planning. The basic

structure of an emergency organisation in Britain was established during the wave of militant industrial unrest which followed the end of the First World War. The use of troops to replace strikers was one main element of the emergencies organisation, or Supply and Transport Organisation as it was called between the wars. Power to deploy troops on civil emergencies was codified in the Emergency Powers Act 1920. The second main element of emergency planning was the use of civilian volunteers. During the 1920s, Volunteer Service Committees (VSCs) were set up across the country to co-ordinate the recruitment and deployment of volunteers during an industrial emergency. (It is ironic that in later years the co-ordinators of volunteers in hospitals were to be called VSCs, given the mistrust of the unions towards the volunteer service committees.) The VSCs were comprised of representatives of government departments and outside organisations with an interest in deploying volunteers during a strike, such as railway and shipping companies. They were chaired by a local person of influence, such as the mayor. The entire organisation was, in theory, secret until the proclamation of an emergency under the Emergency Powers Act 1920, when the Civil Commissioners (who were responsible in Whitehall for operating the scheme) were dispatched to offices in the regions. The preoccupation with secrecy has been a constant feature of emergency planning this century and reflects the concern of successive governments that the emergencies organisation would be seen in trade union eyes as a strike-breaking body.

During the General Strike of May 1926, the VSCs were used to recruit many thousands of volunteers. Independent, non-government organisations also sprang up, such as the Organisation for the Maintenance of Supplies, while the chambers of commerce also played a role in recruitment. From 1926 until the outbreak of the Second World War, the Supply and Transport Organisation was wound down to some extent, although a skeleton organisation was maintained. As for the recruitment of volunteers, a list of suitable chairmen of VSCs was kept up-to-date by the Civil Commissioners' Department and periodic reports were submitted to Whitehall on the position in the regions.[10]

After the war, the Supply and Transport Organisation was reconstituted by the Labour government as the Emergencies Organisation.[11] The immediate postwar years were characterised by a wave of unofficial disputes, especially in the docks and the mines, and troops were introduced on no fewer than 11 separate occasions during the lifetime of the Attlee governments to break strike action.

The government also gave serious consideration to the recruitment of civilian volunteers.

The Attlee government first considered the use of volunteers during an unofficial strike of road haulage drivers in London in January 1947. Troops were brought in to the strike-bound areas to maintain essential supplies but, on 10 January, Ben Smith, the Minister of Food, informed ministers that voluntary assistance would have to be considered if rations were to be maintained. The request was turned down by the Minister of Labour, George Isaacs, who argued that 'such a move would almost certainly be followed by outbursts of industrial unrest all over the country, and the situation might deteriorate almost to the extent of a general strike'.[12]

During the summer of 1947, discussions were held within Whitehall on the possibility of revising the prewar scheme for recruiting volunteers. By June 1948, however, it was clear that these plans had been abandoned by the Home Office.[13] In future, responsibility for the recruitment of volunteers was to rest with the Ministry of Labour and its local offices. This was despite the reservations of the Minister of Labour, who feared that the reputation of the employment exchanges, 'in the eyes of organised labour would be irreparably damaged'.[14]

Between May and July 1949, a nationwide dock strike took place which paralysed Britain's trade. A State of Emergency was declared under the 1920 Act. Troops were brought in to maintain essential supplies and plans were prepared for the recruitment of volunteers. Official papers in the Public Records Office reveal the details of the plans. All volunteers were to be vetted by the Ministry of Labour and classified into one of three groups: skilled in dock machine operation; unskilled, but physically fit for normal manual work; unskilled and fit to undertake light work only. Volunteers were to be employed on a weekly basis with a guaranteed minimum wage for the week. Free accommodation was to be supplied with meals at canteen rates, and overtime rates were to be paid outside normal hours. Protection was to be provided for the volunteers, in an attempt to avoid a repetition of the events of May 1926 when there had been widespread clashes between strikers and volunteers.[15]

Ministers vetoed the call for volunteers on tactical grounds. The fear was that the use of volunteers would antagonise the unions and extend the dispute. The Chief Inspector of the Metropolitan Police warned the government that, although 'the temper of the dockers was excellent and there was no feeling against the use of troops which was taken as a matter of course', the introduction of volunteers 'would cause a lot of feeling among the dockers'.[16]

The election of a Conservative administration in 1951, under Sir Winston Churchill, brought little change to the emergencies organisation. On taking office, the Churchill government did not question the need for a permanent organisation to deal with widespread industrial unrest – its presence was accepted as an integral part of the structure of the modern state, as indeed it has been by governments since.

The decline in large-scale unofficial strikes after 1951, however, did affect the structure of the emergencies organisation. The detailed regional plans, which had been a feature of emergency planning both before the war and after 1945, were not maintained. Troops were called in only once during the lifetime of the Churchill government, to break an unofficial strike of petrol-tanker drivers in London in October 1953. Consideration was given to the deployment of civilian volunteers, but the Minister of Labour, Sir Walter Monckton, opposed the idea on the grounds that volunteers lacked the necessary skills to replace the men on strike, and that their use would risk a serious escalation of the dispute.[17]

In May 1955, the government declared a State of Emergency to deal with a national strike on the railways. A general call for volunteers was not made. The experience of the General Strike had been that enthusiastic volunteers did not necessarily make reliable train drivers. Over the course of the nine days in May 1926, four people were killed and 33 injured due to locomotive crashes involving volunteer drivers. The Emergency Regulations, in 1955, however, did allow for unlicensed individuals to drive buses and trains. The Minister of Transport, Mr Boyd-Carpenter, recalls in his memoirs visiting King's Cross and being told that the only item of news 'was that the Flying Scotsman, with a volunteer driver, was running twenty minutes ahead of time . . .'[18]

Between 1955 and 1966, troops were deployed only once during an industrial dispute, on the occasion of an official seamen's dispute in 1960. It was not until 1966 that a State of Emergency was next declared by Harold Wilson's Labour government during a seven-week strike of seamen. Volunteers were not called for during this period. Despite the fact that it lay dormant for much of the period after 1955, the emergencies organisation, as it had developed after the war, remained intact and largely unaltered until the early 1970s. The miners' strike of 1972 revealed certain inadequacies with the way in which the organisation operated. In particular, it was shown to be incapable of dealing with the increased technical sophistication of industry. Troops and civilian volunteers were found to be of little use as replacement labour for skilled workers in the coal industry, or in the electricity-generating industry. A radical upheaval of the organisation took place. Control over emergency planning was transferred from the Home Office to the Cabinet Office and a new streamlined organisation emerged, the Civil Contingencies Unit, which was to prove effective during the industrial disputes later in the decade.

The history of emergency planning since the war had proved one thing: that civilian volunteers and, indeed for that matter, service personnel, were of little use as replacement labour in a major industrial dispute involving skilled workers. The resurgence of interest, by the Thatcher administration in 1980, in the use of civilian volunteers as strike breakers was thus greeted with scepticism in Whitehall.

However, although it was the case that members of the general public could not be used to replace workers in the mines or in the power stations, white-collar grades within industry could be used to provide volunteer emergency cover. The postwar governments of Clement Attlee and Winston Churchill had looked increasingly to industry to recruit its own volunteer strike breakers. Discussions had been held with the railway companies and shipping companies after the war to persuade them to draw up their own emergency plans. Similarly, in 1980 during a strike of water workers, white-collar staff were used by the water boards to maintain essential services.[19]

Civilian volunteers, moreover, could still be used to replace unskilled workers in the public services. In the early 1980s, a series of strikes broke out in the public services over the government's privatisation programme. Volunteer assistance was called for in a number of cases. In Hammersmith, in June 1984, there was a strike of domestic staff over the decision of the hospital to put cleaning services out to private tender. The newspapers reported that volunteers were used to serve food which had been prepared by managers.[20] In Ulster, in August 1985, a strike of ambulance drivers took place over the use of private taxis. Voluntary ambulance teams were brought in to keep services going.[21]

The Department of Health circular of 1979 had called on health authorities to make advance emergency preparations. In April 1984, confidential notes of a working party set up by the Cornwall and Isles of Scilly Health Authority were leaked to the press. These showed that detailed plans were being prepared to use volunteers to maintain essential supply operations in the event of industrial unrest.[22] The unions were not to be allowed to provide accident or emergency cover during a stoppage and were not to be involved in the contingency planning.

It was not only in the health service that relations between volunteers and unions were put at risk by the provocative use of volunteers. Government cuts in public expenditure during the 1980s, coupled with high levels of unemployment, made unions particularly wary of volunteer involvement. During the long-drawn-out teachers dispute in the mid-1980s, parent volunteers were accused by the teachers' unions of undermining their action. At an annual conference of the National Association of Schoolmasters/Union of Women Teachers, a motion was passed, reminiscent of that passed by COHSE in the early 1970s, attacking the role of volunteer helpers.[23]

A New Partnership

Relations between trade unions and volunteers were at a low ebb in the early 1980s. By the end of the decade, however, there were signs of a lessening of tension. In 1990 five public sector unions, including COHSE and the Transport and General Workers' Union (TGWU), came together with national volunteer-involving organisations to agree a revision of The Volunteer Centre UK's Drain Guidelines and, by the end of the decade, several unions had begun to recruit volunteers into full union membership. The easing of tensions between volunteers and unions was further illustrated during the six-month-long ambulance dispute of 1989–90 when volunteer drivers and ambulance staff in dispute co-operated with each other to maintain an emergency service.

What had brought about this new partnership was a re-evaluation on the part of the Labour movement of the value of voluntary action in society. Two separate factors underpinned Labour's growing support for voluntary action during the 1980s.

First, was the rediscovery of mutual support as an integral part of voluntary action. Mutual support has, of course, always been an essential part of volunteering: Beveridge's seminal work on the structure of voluntary action in Britain after the Second World War highlighted mutual support and philanthropy as the two main ingredients of volunteering. For much of the twentieth century, however, the left in Britain (and, indeed, much of the volunteer movement itself) had ignored mutual support, with the result that volunteering was equated exclusively with philanthropy and charitable good works. This was a strange oversight from the left, as the British Labour movement was founded on the principles of mutual support and collective community action. As the nineteenth century was the century of the philanthropic movements so, too, it saw the birth of mutual aid as a cohesive social force. The friendly societies, the co-operative movement and the trade union movement itself were all born out of voluntary action dedicated to the principle of mutual support. It was the 1960s which first witnessed a resurgence of interest in mutual-aid groups. It was not until the 1980s, however, that the Labour movement began to pay full attention to this movement and to recognise in it a powerful instrument for collective support and social change.

The second factor was a shift in thinking on the left, away from statism towards a 'mixed economy' of welfare, in which the voluntary sector and volunteers were seen to have an important role to play in meeting need in society. Partly, this was a response to a reduction in the power of organised labour during the decade, the consequence of both high unemployment and government policy, which meant that voluntary groups and volunteers (and not Labour) were often in the vanguard of movements for social justice and social change. But it was also the product of a longer process of reassessment on the left of the role of the state in society stretching back more than 20 years.[24] An illustration of this shift in thinking came in 1989 when the Labour Party, as part of its Policy Review programme, set up a working committee of trade unions and voluntary sector representatives to work out a policy on Labour and the voluntary sector. The same year also saw the setting up of Labour Community Action, a pressure group within the Labour Party committed to 'raising awareness of voluntary sector issues in the Labour Party and influencing Labour policy on these issues.'[25]

The prospect for good relations between volunteers and trade unions looks bright as we enter the 1990s, brighter in fact than at any time since the end of the Second World War. Nevertheless, there are trends which threaten to undermine this developing partnership.

One such trend, which became apparent during the last decade, is the blurring of boundaries between paid work and voluntary work (a development looked at in detail in Chapter 1 by Jos Sheard). One cause of this blurring was government special employment measures in the 1980s to deal with large-scale unemployment. Under the Community Programme, for example, unemployed people were engaged in community activities for a nominal wage – activities which, in the past, had often been undertaken by volunteers. The spread of paid volunteer projects in recent years has also contributed to a blurring of boundaries. The unions have opposed such schemes on the grounds that there is little difference between paid volunteers and low-paid workers. However, with organisations finding it increasingly difficult to attract long-term volunteers, the trend towards the payment of volunteers is likely to continue. Contracting out of local authority services through compulsory competitive tendering may also lead to tensions between paid staff and volunteers, especially if organisations (or, indeed, private firms) should be tempted to use volunteers as a source of cheap labour to secure a service contract. Above all, there is the danger that governments, in times of industrial unrest, will use volunteers as a strike-breaking weapon.

CHAPTER 3

DEMOCRACY, VOLUNTARY ACTION AND THE SOCIAL WELFARE SECTOR IN MAINLAND EUROPE

Peter Ely

The Moment of Europhoria

When this book was being planned, it was the impending removal of customs barriers between the 12 countries of the European Community which led British editors to include sections on Europe in their books. But in the final months of 1989, the collapse of communist regimes in East Central Europe and turmoil in the Soviet Union emphasised those achievements of the Community which lay outside the field of international trade.

During the peaceful summer of 1990, there was more awareness of the ways in which the Community had expanded the frontiers of liberty. Conceding liberal capitalism its moment of greatest triumph, the revolutionaries of Eastern Europe had aspired not to some ideological Utopia, but to the flawed but human reality of the kind of society already existing among the Twelve. Political pluralism, market economies and the rule of law were now indisputably identified with modernity, and with affluence.

Other common features of the nations of the Community became more evident. The real measure of a government's success is now considered to be in maintaining liberty and managing the conditions for economic growth, hopefully ending a longstanding emphasis on warfare, domination and empire. National economies are embedded in an international economic system and a measure of affluence is held to be the normal condition of a European, so that those without it feel aggrieved.

Mainland countries of the European Community all have recent experience of fascist despotism, either indigenous, imposed from outside, or a mixture of both. All despotisms, whether fascist or communist, restrict or prohibit citizens from coming together in any association not directly controlled by the ruling party or its supporting groups, and favour compulsory membership of approved organisations.

Community countries now have constitutions with popular legitimacy and support, and some capacity for peaceful internal change. They also have elected local governments and, in the larger countries, regional devolution. There is religious toleration and a formal separation between Church and state, which have a working if sometimes uncomfortable relationship: in every region of the world religious feeling has generated a great deal of voluntary action.

Voluntary Action as Part of the Structure of Democracy

The sociologist of democracy, Alexis de Tocqueville (1805–59), provides a framework for looking at the function of voluntary action in a country's democratic process.[1] Always conscious of the danger that a democracy might deteriorate into a despotism, he felt that the harsh competition in economic life might lead to citizens losing interest in political participation beyond what is necessary to secure their personal financial interests. The rich may want government to provide nothing but law and order, while the less well-off demand only higher incomes and benefits.

If the population loses interest in any concerns wider than trying to turn public policy to their individual advantage, it is likely that a small committed faction will come to power. They, in turn, may strengthen this tendency by any means which enable government to acquire a 'monopoly over public affairs' without limits to its scope or power. They may restrict the circulation of reliable information, and hinder religious bodies who want to proclaim individuals' moral responsibilities towards their fellow citizens. They may limit public education. The opinions of public-minded associations may be labelled subversive.

To prevent this, Tocqueville recommended constitutional arrangements which placed limits on government power. While no laws should be unalterable, constitutional laws should be made difficult to change. A strong judiciary will resist government interference and an effective court system encourages mutual trust between citizens. Local government should have a wide degree of autonomy and so provide widespread opportunities for public participation and training in the democratic process. Religion should not be subject to political control, and all sects should be free to practise. The citizens themselves should be vested with rights, especially those of voting in free elections, freedom of expression and freedom of association.

To be an effective restraint on the government, this 'division of powers' has to be maintained and stabilised by a democratic 'civil society', a term which refers to aspects of society which are not directly political. Democratic civil society is dominated by economic activities, which are generally successful in producing a widely spread prosperity. Because most people own property or possess skills, they feel that they have a stake in the system and are more willing to participate in public affairs.

Individuals are encouraged to satisfy their needs through their own efforts, rather than expecting the political system to supply them with everything. But people follow an 'enlightened self-interest', which enables them to transcend purely selfish concerns. This attitude is maintained by the free flow of ideas, by public education policy, and by religious influences.

It is difficult for an individual to accomplish much in public affairs by acting alone. But many citizens possess the ability to organise groupings which pursue shared interests in an orderly fashion. These voluntary associations combat both competitive attitudes between citizens and the tendency for government to over-extend its powers. They assert the right of such groups to circulate information concerning their area of interest, to facilitate discussion and to make the weight of their views publicly known. In short, the right to believe that they may 'know better' than the government in their special area, to become alternative centres of social power, of public concern, knowledge and expertise in competition with the government, or in co-operation with it.

Voluntary associations do not arise automatically from a democratic civil society, but must be created by the concerted efforts of many individuals and sustained by the other rights and conditions of democratic life. They offer a training ground for participation, for acquiring the skills of leadership and a familiarity with the general political process. They have formally elected officials, rules which limit the power of the executive, and accountability of officials to the membership.

Associations enable members to experience friendly and co-operative relations and feelings of solidarity through participation in a common undertaking. Tocqueville considered that it is inter-personal trust which most needs to be diffused among the people of a democracy, in contrast to the authoritarian style of personal interaction, mutual suspicion and hostility deliberately fostered by despotic governments. It could be added, therefore, that actions by individual volunteers, not in association, also contribute to demo-cratic social relations if they express interpersonal solidarity.

In the following pages we shall look at voluntary action in specific countries from the perspective of Tocqueville's analysis of its place in a democracy.

The Federal Republic of Germany, 1945 to 1990

As Conradt points out,[2] the most carefully constructed constitution is of little value if the society and culture are not supportive of its key principles and norms. The prewar Weimar Republic had all the formal structures of political democracy, but it was a 'republic without republicans', as most Germans longed for a strong authoritarian government of either a right- or a left-wing nature, so that the degree of consensus needed for a democratic system did not exist. Thus Hitler rose to power by constitutional means before he proceeded to eliminate every legally safeguarded civil liberty.

The West German constitution (Basic Law) imposed by the Western occupying powers was deliberately designed to prevent another return to despotism by constitutional means. Once again the constitutional structures of democracy were in place, but would Germans accept and support these constitutional structures, remain indifferent, or even embrace anti-democratic ideologies and move-ments? The constitution-writers left power in the hands of political élites and saw public participation as being limited to formal events, such as voting in elections.

In the immediate postwar period there was widespread withdrawal from public and political matters and an exclusive concern with family survival. But by 1985 a quarter of the population had an affiliation with a political party and society was honeycombed with associations at all levels: there were 250,000 voluntary associations and a further 22,120 independent self-help groups. Successive public-opinion polls revealed a significantly increasing proportion of the public conceding legitimacy to the West German constitution and acknowledging the value of party-political conflict in a democracy. They had also come to believe that parliamentary representatives are concerned with the general public interest rather than solely with their personal or party interest. Together with the growth in affluence, an anti-authoritarian democratic outlook had emerged.

We can trace the history of voluntary action in the health and welfare sector as a part of this development. The Federal Republic of West Germany was a welfare state, in that any individual unable to cope with adverse circumstances who did not receive sufficient help from his or her family was entitled to assistance. But this should be directed, if possible, to restoring their capacity to help themselves. Furthermore, the West German Basic Law, which is now the constitution of united Germany, specifies the maximum dispersal and delegation of governmental powers. What individuals and families can do for themselves should not be supplanted by church or other welfare organisations. Municipalities should not intervene unless these independent welfare organisations cannot cope or are not interested in meeting the need. The state (*Land*) government should not intervene unless the municipality is similarly incapable, nor should the federal authorities supplant the state government.

This is the principle of 'subsidiarity', that is, the maximum dispersal and delegation of powers, which is most developed in Catholic thought, though a parallel idea of 'separate spheres' is found in Calvinist thinking of the same period.[3] The encyclical *Rerum Novarum*, issued by Pope Leo XIII in 1891, laid down strict limits to the right of the state to intervene in the affairs of the individual and family. On the fortieth anniversary of this encyclical, Pius XI issued *Quadragesimo Anno* which stated that no larger or higher organisation should take over the functions which can be adequately performed by smaller and lower societies:

> ... once flourishing human society and the varieties of different forms of association have been destroyed to the extent that finally there exists only the state and the individual ... Government, which has taken over all the tasks and functions formerly carried out by different and now displaced associations has been strangled by the overwhelming burden of obligations and responsibilities ...[4]

In accordance with the 'subsidiarity' principle, there is no equivalent to the British National Health Service, but more than 90 per cent of the former West German population is covered by one of hundreds of health insurance schemes organised on a local, guild, trade union or other basis, to whose funds an independently practising medical profession can alone authorise access. Unemployment relief is a matter for the municipal governments. And in the welfare field the powers of the federal government are limited to research and experimental projects, though it funds some provision indirectly through charitable foundations. The state's direct services are mainly confined to those fields directly connected to legal sanctions, while the so-called 'Big Six' independent welfare associations account for the bulk of welfare expenditure. These are the Roman Catholic association Caritas (Deutscher Caritasverband), the Protestant welfare association (Diakonisches Werk der Evangelischen Kirche in Deutschland), the Workers' welfare association (Arbeiterwohlfahrt), the German Red Cross (Deutsches Rotes Kreuz), the Jewish welfare association (Zentrale Wohlfahrtsstelle der Juden in Deutschland), and the Non-Denominational welfare association (Deutscher Paritätischer Wohlfahrtsverband). The three largest of these alone employ 580,000 people full-time or 2.7 per cent of the employed workforce.[5]

The Weimar Republic had recognised a similar group of associations for welfare delivery purposes.[6] On coming to power, the Nazis reasoned that the Weimar welfare state would support the idle and assist those 'unfit for life'. Voluntary welfare associations were banned or suppressed or, as with the German Red Cross, assimilated into the Nazi machine. Voluntarism became an instrument of Nazi mass mobilisation and fund-raising campaigns, and the National Socialist Nation's Welfare Association became the largest mass organisation in the Third Reich.

After the Second World War, the financial position of the churches was secured by the imposition of a 'church tax', a surcharge of 10 per cent on the individual's income tax, collected by the tax authorities and passed on to the churches at no charge to them. This was in accordance with the Allies' aim of strengthening non-governmental organisations.

But there is no strong tradition of separation between church and state and the Big Six are deeply embedded in the state structure. They are frequently described as state-oriented rather than market-oriented, and many committee members at national, state (*Land*) and municipal levels hold power through offices in the national political parties. Siebel[7] characterises them as top-down organisations due to the strength of the central direction of the national associations and their party linkages. Far from being in competition with government or even with each other, tasks are distributed among the 'Big Six' through a process of permanent bargaining between state authorities, political parties and welfare associations, supported by a strong consensus on welfare.

During the late 1960s, West Germany went through a crisis of participation and an anti-authoritarian movement which involved a shift from traditionally passive forms of political participation. The Big Six were criticised for over-professionalisation and for the fragmentation and specialisation of their services. It was felt that they were too bureaucratic and alienated their clients from helpers. 'Help' was misused as a means of social control, clients were placed in a position of child-like dependence, and the associations were administering suffering rather than fighting it. In addition, they were said to be showing inflexibility towards new needs, especially those of elderly people for domiciliary help rather than residential care, and not taking into account new personal attitudes of self-management and self-confidence.[8]

From the early 1970s, tens of thousands of 'citizens' initiatives' arose. Encouraged at first by the Social Democratic Party, they soon took on a larger life of their own involving the peace, anti-nuclear and green movements, and they are now current throughout the German-language area, that is, Germany, Austria, Luxembourg and eastern Switzerland. Some are devoted to public action on a single issue. But there are also groups which carry out tasks themselves. These 'self-help' groups are either self-help in the therapeutic sense of being made up of sufferers from a common condition, or in terms of themselves managing a service which they provide to the public. There are also groups in the 'alternative movement', either concerned with the environment or with the long-term reconstruction of society, and groups in the consumers' movement.[9]

In the health and welfare field, the medical profession has generally been willing to authorise insurance-fund finance for self-help or self-management groups whom they regard as assisting their patients, or enhancing patient co-operation. The public authorities have also been receptive to this voluntary action as a hopefully cheaper and more cost-effective means of meeting need. The federal government set up six information clearing houses to assist them, and several state (*Land*) governments established special budgets and research projects. They enjoy the support of the four major parties, but not of the trade unions.

Anxious that they might be displaced, or that a number of these initiatives might come together to form a 'Big Seventh', the Big Six independents agreed together that one of their number, the Non-Denominational welfare association (Deutscher Paritätischer Wohlfahrtsverband), should offer an umbrella organisation for the newcomers. Thus these new groups are now part of a four-way power struggle between themselves, the six large independents trying to show that they are 'better' organisations by incorporating them, a public administration looking for economies, and the medical profession.[10]

How this works at the local level can be seen in the town and district of Lüneburg in Lower Saxony.[11] Applications to come under the local Non-Denominational umbrella have to be approved at meetings of the Big Six at state (*Land*) level, and are vetoed if they are considered a 'front for commercial interests' or duplicate an existing service, producing competition. The 27 member organisations in Lüneburg vary widely in size and scope. One provides a complete range of psychiatric services for the town, another runs an equally comprehensive set of services for old people. Others are small, providing one or two residential homes, a workshop, kindergarten, therapeutic community, sail training ship, counselling, or tea room. There are a number of clubs for lonely people, and for those diagnosed as having a particular illness or problem. Only one organisation has primarily consciousness-raising objectives, in the field of mental health. The extent to which they make use of unpaid volunteers is equally variable. It is often at the stage of becoming a more formal organisation, or a service provider, that such groups join the umbrella. Many others are wary of identification with the Big Six.

To help the groups which become members, the Lower Saxony organisation of the Non-Denominational Deutscher Paritätischer Wohlfahrtsverband umbrella deploys 10 departments which are expert on different client groups or therapeutic approaches, and a sector offering advice on management, finance, personnel, public relations, and representative structures. A considerable weight of professionalisation is thus brought to bear. On the other hand, these new groups have helped to exert pressure on the Big Six to adapt from the inertia of their cartel and to develop new emphases, such as de-institutionalisation. The Workers' welfare association (Arbeiterwohlfahrt) has extended itself to encourage ethnically based associations among 'guest workers' and, since before reunification unemployment was most severe in Protestant north Germany, the Protestant welfare association (Diakonisches Werk) developed work to alleviate poverty.

The extent to which the Big Six make use of volunteers is variable.

They are most evident in the Red Cross where they meet the social needs of hospital patients. Others of the Six recruit young people of a good academic standard to make up staff shortfalls. They are then used as unpaid labour as a prelude to offering them paid employment or before they go on to professional training in universities or polytechnics.[12] In the past three years, on a federal initiative, a network of *Sozialstationen* has been set up on a ratio of one per 30,000 population as bases for generating more volunteer help for the domiciliary care of chronically sick and frail elderly people. Hardworking volunteers are to be given recognition through financial awards. Consortia of two, three, or four of the Big Six, depending on the locality, have secured the implementation of this project in order to avoid competition among themselves. But they have encountered much difficulty in tapping into the hypothetical reservoir of volunteers, either because it does not exist, or through problems in their approach. The *Sozialstationen* are regarded by the public more as forums for co-operation between paramedicals and social workers.

This glimpse of one sector of voluntary action in the former West Germany has shown initiatives growing up alongside the old hierarchical structures. These new groups are often very discriminating about what they identify with, frequently embody demands for participation in the policy-making process, and seek to form a more flexible and responsive democracy. In the Green Party, this has expressed itself at the national level as an attempt to form a party of the left which is concerned with modern issues, such as the environment and equal rights.

Spain

As Hooper[13] suggests, in some respects Spain has less securely emerged from despotism into modern democratic Europe than had West Germany. The economy is less developed, affluence is less widely spread, and the proportion of the population in middle-class occupations is lower. Internal threats to democracy can still be assumed to exist. But political, economic and social progress since the death of Franco in 1975 has been considerable.

Among a multitude of reforms, the policy to grant regional autonomy can be mentioned for taking much of the heat out of the 'nationality question' and for enabling energy to be devoted to economic development. The German Social Democratic Party has significantly assisted the ruling Partido Socialista Obrero Español (PSOE) with finance and advice about how to emerge from fascism.

Under the dictatorship, Spain went through the 'years of hunger' during the Second World War and after. The United Nations imposed a trade embargo up to 1950. Serious unrest in 1957 led Franco to appoint 'technocrats' to the Trade and Industry Ministry, who piloted the country through the 'years of development' from 1961 to 1973. During this period, the remittances of expatriate Spaniards, foreign investment and the phenomenal growth of the tourist industry, allowed Spain to benefit at second hand from the economic boom in democratic countries. Internal migration to the cities during the 'hunger' and 'development' periods freed most Spaniards from the feudal political relationships of the countryside and, together with economic development, laid the foundations of the new Spain.

During the dictatorship there was a general prohibition on association between citizens. The Movimiento Nacional was the only legal political party, and the only voluntary organisations permitted were the Red Cross and the Catholic organisation Caritas, created in 1942. The failure of the Spanish Church to absorb new ideas had led to anti-clericalism being identified with radicalism, and Catholicism being over-identified with the reactionary, affluent ruling class. During the civil war (1936–39), the Church supported Franco and anti-Franco forces burned down churches and killed over 4,000 parish priests.

In the early years of the dictatorship, Caritas worked closely with the government, being mainly concerned with 'social auxiliary' work distributing food and clothing received from international sources. But in the technocratic era, the research carried out by a Caritas-sponsored foundation made a significant contribution to the social aspects of economic planning. The Church itself was changing. The death or exile of so many Freemasons, Anarchists and Marxists during the civil war and the Franco era had provided an unprecedented freedom of manoeuvre, and several missions set up to help the working class aroused the conscience of both laity and clergy. Deeply influenced by the liberal spirit flowing from the Second Vatican Council, in the 1970s bishops began criticising the regime. So many priests were imprisoned that a special prison was opened for them.

Today, the PSOE is increasingly attracting Catholic voters and members. In 1986, 45 per cent were 'believers'. The democratic constitution of 1978 guaranteed the right to associate, but a spontaneous proliferation of voluntary action has not yet taken place. The largest associations remain the Red Cross and Caritas.

The Spanish Caritas Federation today considers itself to be the active conscience of the Church, carrying out the third of the latter's threefold mission of worship, teaching and charity. But social justice has overtaken simplistic interpretations of charity, and Caritas is organised around ideas rather than the provision of material help. Caritas undertakes research on the extent and the causes of the problems facing poor people, and presents the information to the public in order to hold them and the government to their responsibilities. It regards itself as collaborating with the government, but also critical of it.

Caritas carries out 15 nationwide programmes providing services which are either complementary to state provision, or which fill gaps where no state services exist. These programmes help old people, mothers, migrants, gypsies, families, children and drug dependants, provide disaster assistance and undertake community action. In all of them, it simultaneously carries out 'cultural action' using the methods of the Brazilian educationalist, Paolo Freire. Eschewing all dogmatism, whether of the left or the right, Freire taught through a dialogue with his students designed to develop not only their knowledge of the world, but their awareness of the way in which they perceived it. This imparted a habit of thinking which through being a 'perpetual dialogue between objectivity and subjectivity' undermined rigidity of all kinds. Caritas does not just offer help, but helps poor people to help themselves.

Caritas thus combats *insolaridad*, the disinclination to associate in the public interest and the tendency of people to limit their horizons to their own selfish interests. Caritas calls upon the services of 27,000 volunteers. Many of these work in their professional capacity as medical or social workers, and may have a lifetime's association with the movement which sometimes only comes to full fruition on their retirement when they have more time to spare. It also has 1,559 salaried employees and is organised on a parish or inter-parish basis, though with financial autonomy from the Church. Using TV and radio, it runs a distance-training programme for volunteers and for self-help.

The government, encumbered with unjust, underfunded and badly organised social insurance and welfare provisions, put its early efforts into creating some state services. Now faced with a financial crisis, it has tried to develop small local associations to which it can contract out tasks, such as the care of elderly people, to volunteers who may receive a token payment. With the growth of this contract culture, an increasing impatience with Caritas's consciousness-raising activities has developed. In 1989 government support to Caritas was severely reduced, the Minister of Social Affairs alleging that she was better served by the Red Cross. In response, Caritas threatened to take the government to the constitutional court for breach of its duty to protect associations. This public confrontation was put into abeyance by a promise to restore funding in the subsequent year. But it marked Caritas's transition from an association embedded in government to one in competition with it, and had resonances for the protection of the poor and their democratic future, the separation of Church and state, and the power of the Church in Spain.

Italy

Italy became a united country against the opposition of the Holy See, which refused to recognise the new state and carried on its charitable and educational work in isolation from it. The parliamentary franchise was very restricted and in Tuscany a voluntary association, Pubblica Assistenza, was formed to provide services and to struggle for political rights for those excluded from the political process. After the First World War, the franchise was extended and, in the 1922 elections, two genuinely mass parties, Catholic and socialist, won half the seats between them. To avoid the democratic outcome of this result, the former ruling élite offered power to Mussolini who proceeded to dismantle the constitution.

Unwilling to face a head-on collision, Mussolini and the Vatican signed the Lateran Pact, which resolved the territorial question by recognising the Vatican as a sovereign state and granted the Church important financial and educational privileges. In return, the Church agreed to disband its political party and instead greatly expanded its lay organisations, principally Azione Cattolica, which was the only legal alternative to fascism and nurtured the future ruling élite. After the Second World War, the leaders of the separate Catholic, socialist and communist resistance forces became the new political leaders and drew up a democratic constitution, article two of which embodies the right to free association.

Sassoon[14] points out that since then Italy, in the north at least, has followed the same path of socio-economic development as other Western European countries, but its political situation – with the Christian Democratic Party permanently in power, and political

Catholicism and communism competing for dominance – is not found elsewhere in the West. But Italian communism differs crucially from the orthodox version in that its philosopher, Gramsci, wrote of building alliances between classes, it has never advocated a command economy, and it came to accept that Italy is a part of the West.

To compete with the Catholic parish organisation, the communists extended their organisation in such a way that they became a genuine mass party instead of the usual group of committed conspirators. But the outcome of this competition was that virtually no aspect of civil society was placed outside the political sphere. Banks, insurance companies, the civil service, and trade unions became extensions of political parties, as did sporting clubs, cultural, leisure-time and pressure groups, and other forms of voluntary action.

An outstanding exception was Pubblica Assistenza, which re-assembled after near-total suppression by Mussolini to provide a forum through which Catholics, socialists and communists could co-operate at a local level to provide paramedical services, disaster relief and community development.

At first the Vatican intervened directly in Italian politics to prevent the emergence of a second, left-wing Catholic party, and to forbid the faithful to support or co-operate with the communists. But in 1961, Pope John XXIII's encyclical *Mater et Magistra* began to question the support being given by the Church to capitalism, and in 1963 *Pacem in Terris* made a distinction between 'false ideologies' (communism and Marxism) and the political movements they inspire, which may embody just and worthy demands. Dialogue between believers and non-believers may produce truth. In 1967 Paul VI issued *Populorum Progressio* which declared that a system which puts the pursuit of private profit, competition and the absolute right to private property at the centre of its beliefs was incompatible with Christian principles. In 1971 *Octogesima Adveniens* asserted that no social system could be derived from the social doctrine of the Church. Christians could thus be active in any political party, which marked a parting of the ways between the Vatican and the Christian Democrats. The Church was freed to project itself as an international body whose function was providing religious not political answers to human problems.

The Second Vatican Council acknowledged the distinctive contri-bution that the laity could make to the Church, which was no longer to be the exclusive prerogative of the clergy. Azione Cattolica became more democratic, more independent of the clergy, and more religious than political. Other lay associations severed their links with the

Christian Democrats, and Catholics set up associations outside party or Church control. During 1970–77, the Italian women's movement – centred on unstructured consciousness-raising groups within, as well as outside, Catholic associations – was dominant in campaigns to legalise divorce, then abortion. The Christian Democrats opposed and were defeated in these struggles, but the Vatican remained neutral, more concerned to preserve Church unity. During the same period, anti-authoritarian youth movements became involved in single-issue campaigns in defence of marginalised groups outside the organised working class, such as prisoners and psychiatric patients.

In recognition of the growth of welfare state services, in 1977 the Church transferred some of its hospitals and universities to the state. A new approach was growing in the Catholic charitable networks which remained, and in the numerous voluntary groups now spontaneously burgeoning in the health and welfare sectors. These embody a wish to meet the non-material needs of service users by forming a relationship and showing solidarity with them. They also encompass a belief that voluntarism incorporates values superior to those of the state services, by understanding problems from the users' point of view and through democratic working methods. Such values enable voluntary action to influence policy at regional or local level because those concerned with a particular problem can be mobilised.

In the south, where the economy is less developed and much employment is in the state sector, the traditional Catholic philan-thropic networks are still the main vehicles for voluntary action, receiving little government funding and with few contacts with local government, whose services are said to have no credibility.[15]

But in the north, surveys have shown that there are over 3 million active volunteers. Forty per cent of the thousands of voluntary associations were started after 1977, and the majority of them are small, with a well-defined local territory. They increasingly involve themselves in the provision of personal social services. At first, they met with opposition from those employed in local government who feared for their jobs, but involvement with voluntary action is now regarded as a safeguard against service reductions. Provision through voluntary action is politically convenient, popular and perhaps cheaper and more efficient. It is coming to be seen as a third alternative, differing from both market forces and state monopoly services.

Increasing numbers of voluntary associations are funded by local government through the *convenzióne* system, whereby the association contracts to provide a service in return for funding, but is free to organise the provision as it likes within the limits of the Italian constitution, which bans religious or other forms of discrimination.[16] As they enter into these partnerships, there is a tendency for groups to become more formally organised, and to rely less on volunteer help. There is a tension between the need to guard their independence and their co-operative but critical stance towards state policies, and the desire of government to use them as mere instruments for delivering services. Voluntary action contributes both to taking local and regional welfare services out of party politics, and to the energy of political life at these levels.

The Netherlands

The Dutch state is also guided by 'subsidiarity' (see page 50), in that the bulk of services are provided through independent organisations. These and society in general are still largely divided into separate 'pillars'. Originally a method for allowing Protestants and Catholics to live side by side, 'pillarisation' meant that 'the choice of which social organisations to join, which political party to vote for, which school to send their children to, became a simple one of religion'.[17] People lived within a coherent network of social, cultural, educational and political organisations. During the 1920s, a third, socialist or 'neutral' pillar was added to the other two and, in the 1960s, new associations claimed that they belonged to a humanist or a liberal pillar.

After the Second World War, a movement for national unity, 'Breakthrough', tried to modify the way in which social and political life was fragmented and divided into compartments. But after nearly a decade of 'Breakthrough', the leaders of the religious pillars once more tried to restrict contact between the hierarchically organised pillars to themselves – a policy in which they persisted until 1965. The hostile public response weakened 'pillarisation' and, during the 1960s, many new associations organised in a democratic and participative way were formed. These devoted themselves to single issues, or were part of movements outside the pillar structure, and relied wholly on volunteer effort or on securing government funding.

A high proportion of the population undertakes voluntary action. Five million people do volunteer work out of a population of 14 million.[18] The proliferation of associations, the general affluence and the extreme libertarianism which characterises the urban centres, in contrast with the extreme conservatism in both Catholic and

Calvinist rural areas, have all contributed to the 'ungovernability' of the Netherlands. The central government, overwhelmed by demands for assistance from too many special interests, too much pluralism, has reacted in two ways. Local and provincial governments have been strengthened at the expense of the 'pillars', by being given budgetary responsibility for social services. Thus associations have to attune their services to local needs when making their case for financial support, and show that they conform to municipal plans. The local governments' powers to set up their own services to compete with the independent associations have also been extended, though seldom acted upon because of the financial crisis.

At the national level, the government has refused to deal with three or more national organisations, defined by religion or ideology, for every client group. It has therefore insisted on amalgamations between the 'pillars' as a condition of recognition, on the grounds that users' needs should predominate over ideology. It has also struck a blow against the hierarchical nature of certain associations by insisting on internal 'democratisation' as a condition of funding, involving client and employee councils which can nominate individuals to management boards.[19]

Ploeg[20] considers that it is no longer possible to clearly differentiate between government and independent associations, owing to the budgetary and organisational controls imposed and also because of the 'privatisation' of some municipal services. A similar blurring occurs in the field of voluntary work as opposed to unpaid work, or even paid work.[21] Among unemployed people, volunteer work has become a step towards getting a job. Volunteers tend to be employed on similar duties as paid staff, to aspire to similar standards of performance, and to be well protected by training, insurance and expenses payments.

A Single Path?

Voluntary action in southern Italy, Spain, northern Italy, the former West Germany, and the Netherlands could be placed at different points along a similar path of development on which Portugal and perhaps Greece could also be located. Each country provides a unique social and historical environment, but everywhere voluntary action has developed along with affluence. As voluntary action has grown, it has separated itself from its identification with existing political parties and from the politics of religion. This expansion has also been assisted by the fact that the religious authorities, too, have distanced themselves from political parties. As the voluntary sector has extended civil society at the expense of political society, contesting its field of action on the grounds of the formal and substantive rights of service users rather than of political ideology, associations have become formally secularised and less driven by ideology.

As associations enter into relations with government, they become more formally organised and less reliant on voluntary labour. Large establishment organisations, a long way from their roots in voluntarism, tend to use volunteers in a utilitarian way. They are vulnerable to challenges to their values from new voluntary groups and even from governments demanding value for money, rights for users and non-discriminatory service delivery.

Other countries do not readily fit the above pattern. Belgium, like France, has been engaged in decentralising a formerly centralised democracy, but lack of available material precludes any discussion of voluntary action there. France and the Scandinavian countries, which are analysed below, do not lend themselves so readily as those already discussed to an analysis on the 'separation of powers' model which Tocqueville advocated (see pages 47–9).

France

The extreme centralisation of the French state around the time of Louis XIV has persisted through several revolutionary changes from monarchy to republic and empire, and back again. The dominant form of republicanism has historically been Jacobinism, which outlawed all associations which came between the citizen and the state, and a general 'right of association' was not granted until 1901. France is generally described as a state stronger than society, and political discourse generally fails to stress any differentiation between the two, since in rhetorical terms the people are the state and have identical interests.

There has been a general consensus in support of the state's prerogatives, for different reasons, among political parties, and hence no stable tradition or routine pattern of relationships with voluntary action, whose legitimacy is never beyond question.[22] There is a tendency on the part of government to claim that it has a wider democratic mandate and ultimate responsibility, and can thus appeal to higher values than unelected groups. French bureaucrats have a highly developed sense that they alone represent the public interest. Their objective is to obtain information rather than to receive advice, and they view the excessive involvement of interest groups as endangering both democracy and the 'objective' resolution of a problem.[23] History has predisposed people to look to the state to resolve problems, rather than to private enterprise or voluntary action.

In addition, there is a tendency to measure political reality against abstract ideas and hence to be cynical about political life. Thus people are inclined to resort to mass actions, sometimes violent, as a means of political participation.

Unlike the constitutions of Germany, Spain, or Italy, that of the Fifth Republic was adopted in reaction to ineffective government, not dictatorship, and incorporates a strong executive presidency and a parliament with diminished powers. Since the first decade of this century, the state has been determinedly secular, and anti-clericalism remains widespread. Catholicism has been historically identified with monarchism and reaction, and it was not until 1945 that a Catholic party, Mouvement républicain populaire (MRP) emerged with fully republican credentials. While some priests fought with the Resistance, senior figures in the Church had compromised themselves with the far right, and in 1990 a known war criminal was found still concealed in a French monastery.

All these factors have contributed to a situation where affluence has not been followed by a proliferation of voluntary action. While surveys show that informal exchanges of voluntary help are widespread, particularly between relatives, the number of voluntary associations has increased, but not to a remarkable extent.[24] Rather than being general throughout society, voluntary action in association with others is the work of small but committed groups of *militants associatifs*.

But, of course, there are some positive elements. France is enjoying constitutional stability, having managed to accommodate having different political parties in power, and 'cohabitation' between a president and a prime minister of different parties. During the 1970s, the women's movement united several existing organisations previously tied to political parties and, in a sustained campaign, won improvements to women's formal and substantive rights. On a longer time-span, in 1947 a group of Catholic trade unionists broke away from the communist-inspired general confederation to set up its own confederation, the Confédération française démocratique du travail (CFDT), which became the second largest. In 1964 they secularised themselves and, though initially close to the MRP, they decided not to become the paymasters of their own political party (the British solution), but to contest the parties' and the state's monopoly of public affairs.

In 1965 the CFDT launched the idea of *autogestion* (self-management) which is 'not one of those mobilising myths which evokes little save unattainable aspirations'. Rather it indicates how a grass-roots movement discovers what needs to be changed and how it should be done, by starting from specific practical situations. It is both a method and a direction of social change, via 'a kind of pedagogical method which consists of launching ideas, accepting them as such and then gradually going more deeply into them, devising ways of applying them, living them and achieving them'.[25]

During the 1970s, *autogestion* drew in ecologists and representatives of the eight national minorities protesting about 'colonialism' within France, the dominance of Paris and of French-speakers, and the Socialists drew deeply on its ideas to secure the presidency in 1981. Legislation followed which regionalised education, and established worker representation on factory management boards. The government set up special structures to relate to the voluntary sector.

Continuing measures to decentralise power to local government are driven not so much by *autogestion* as by the impatience of the mayors of the great French cities with the supervision of the *préfects*, officials who managed local administration for the Interior Ministry. Devolution to *communes* and *départements*, and the grouping of the latter into regions, continued in 1986. The *préfects* have now been renamed *commissaires de la République*, and given a block grant for *départemental* affairs which must be apportioned by local negotiation. But the simultaneous holding of up to three elected offices at different local and national levels by the same politican, and the tendency of top civil servants to hold important local elective offices, militates against separating localised interests from central ones. The 'separation of powers' is always a problem in France and the attachment of the alienating and authoritarian French political culture to representative rather than participatory democracy may have ensured that *autogestion* is a long-term project.

Nevertheless, while devolution may be criticised on the grounds that it has everything except public participation, research has shown that local services are now less compartmentalised and more 'open' to democratic influences.[26] Moreover, *départemental* social services and communes increasingly support associations providing day services for old people or children which may employ salaried workers, but are administered by committees of volunteers.

Voluntary associations in France tend to be either embedded in the administrative apparatus or to be in outright competition with it. As regards the former, concepts like government 'managing the forces available within associative life'[27] make it clear that the administration has a hierarchical idea of co-operation between the public and 'private' sectors. (The term *privé* includes everything which is not public, hence both voluntary and commercial sectors.) But the expansion of the voluntary sector has enlarged the number of centres where decisions can be made, and hence improved flexibility.

How this works at a local level, can be seen in the example of an association for social action in the socially deprived conurbation of Dunkirk, the Association Educative de la Flandre Intérieure et Maritime, known as the 'Association Educative'.[28] In 1988 this had a budget of 30 million francs drawn from the areas of responsibility of five government ministries, and employed 186 people who were 'volunteers' only to the extent that they might have gained higher remuneration in the public or for-profit sectors.

With financial operations devolved to the co-operative bank and a decentralised style of management, six members of staff at the association's headquarters co-ordinate a range of children's homes which are designated by both the justice and social/health bureaucracies for the use of the children's judge, whose capacity to dispense justice is enhanced by not having to rely on a monopoly of public provision. So that the children may have contact with animals, the municipality has provided a small farm. The association also runs large-scale employment training for building tradesmen and car mechanics. Funding for two detached youth organisers has been secured from the *département* without reference to the municipality, which preferred to give the prevention of delinquency a low profile.

The Association Educative had taken another initiative by setting up another association which drew together elected politicians, prominent citizens, key members of associations and relevant officials to provide various types of practical help to people who were homeless or in precarious housing situations. It was also the leading member of a 'collective' of caring organisations in Dunkirk for discussing issues of common interest. Among these, it was the only organisation solely based in Dunkirk, the others being branches of national or international organisations, such as the Red Cross and the Salvation Army.

But membership of this Dunkirk collective extended from these

service providers across to associations who compete with government in a way which reproaches it with the fact that poor people do
not have the economic rights which would enable them to exercise
their political rights or rights to live a secure family life. Among these
are some associations founded by charismatic leaders which operate
throughout the French-language area (France, southern Belgium
and western Switzerland), depend heavily on volunteer work and
approach financial self-sufficiency. Emmaus, a community of social
rejects supporting itself by waste recycling and the sale of second-
hand goods donated by the public, was founded by Abbé Pierre, as a
call to altruism and to people in rich countries not to forget the poor.
Another priest, J. Wresinsky, founded ATD Fourth World, in which
teams of volunteers live in very poor neighbourhoods to provide help
to families. Harlem Désir leads SOS–Racisme, which provides
animation (a form of community organisation indigenous to France)
to minority groups, financed by anti-racist concerts. The actor
Coluche founded Restaurants of the Heart to provide millions of
meals to poor people, and was the most influential of all through his
skill in using the media to raise consciousness and bring home the
message that there is still hunger amidst the general affluence.
Coluche inspired a significant increase in volunteering and in
philanthropic giving, for which he helped to secure fiscal incentives.[29]

Norway, Denmark and Sweden

These countries are marked by affluence, small populations, a
profound social conformity, and by a collectivist political culture in
which legislation is often preceded by years of consultation so that the
resulting policies have a broad base of support. As concepts, society
and the state are not strongly differentiated. There is a high level of
welfare state expenditure and the services are highly professionalised.

The culture strongly supports associations, so that total membership of these may exceed the total population. Boli[30] describes
associations in Sweden as having three main activities: social reform,
recreation and personal development, and the defence of organised
interests.

In the social services field there are associations of staff of the
services, of consumers, and some organised around fields of interest.
But with very few exceptions, these associations provide no services
themselves. They tend to be dominated by their professional
employees whose research teams publish material which raises the

level of information and debate. People join them routinely as an aspect of their job or condition. They are subsidised by, and work in close co-operation with, the government, and are rarely involved in fund-raising for welfare from non-state sources. Thus taxation pays for both services and participation.

In return for its money, the state gets a policy input at the policy-formulation phase. In Sweden, association representatives also sit on the 'lay boards' which monitor state services, and association 'assessors' sit with judges in the housing, labour, and market courts.

The comparison by Selle and Øymyr[31] of associations in a Norwegian province in 1941 with the situation in 1988, demonstrates changes in associational life arising from the growth of the welfare state. They found an increase from one association per 49 inhabitants to one per 33. Missionary and teetotal associations, 'once the strongest mass movements in Norwegian history', had declined, though religious groups had developed numerous youth and sports associations. Social and humanitarian associations – previously small, all-female groups presumably providing neighbourly help – now included substantial male representation. They also tended to extend across a wider geographical area, interact with the local authority, be concerned with public policy, co-operate with other local associations, and be branches of national organisations.

In Norway about 38 per cent of health and social service provision is channelled through independent, mostly Lutheran Church associations. Many of these were founded in 1960–75. Policy was largely indifferent as to the relative merits of direct or indirect state provision, but indirect provision was cost-effective as the organisations already possessed valuable resources, such as building sites.[32] The hand of the state has not been very intrusive in the running of these agencies, but they have undergone internal tensions and changes in line with a general secularisation of society, so that religious aims have been distinguished from therapeutic ones. The professional staff tend to emerge as the dominant influence.

Denmark saw little reason to channel services via the state Church, and has historically preferred direct state services. If a voluntary association developed new services, it would be with the objective that government should absorb them, and voluntary action was thus regarded as the sign of a deficiency in state provision.

There was no government interest in volunteering until 1982 when the fiscal crisis brought a conservative government to power. A central bureau was set up whose director writes of self-reliance, subsidiarity, and a pluralism of provision.[33] Nevertheless, she envisages the involvement of volunteer groups in the care of old people only to the extent that they will provide friendship, and read or tell stories to them. If such groups tried to provide other services, they would meet opposition from the professional associations, and anyone wanting to help an old person further would best do so as an individual.

But voluntary action is by no means completely absorbed into the state bureaucracy and reliance on professionalised state services is not complete. The Church Cross Army behaves like a non-Scandinavian voluntary association in raising money and making use of volunteer labour in providing preventive, counselling and rehabilitative services for people who abuse alcohol. Organisations of the Lutheran and other churches give financial and material help to the very poor, and guide them through the welfare bureaucracy, financing these operations largely through the sale of second-hand clothes. The volunteers who read and tell stories to old people are also frequently church-based. But perhaps the major part of Scandinavian philanthropy is directed at the poor of other countries, leaving the state and its professionals to care for the Scandinavian poor.

The personal initiative of a teacher, J. Petersen, has led to a national network of groups of people suffering from common diagnoses, which are self-help in the therapeutic sense. Members of the large formal users' associations organise telephone and personal contact groups among themselves.

In Sweden the delivery of virtually all services by direct state provision has not been significantly challenged, and it is probably the only Western European country not to offer any tax concessions for philanthropic giving. Gould[34] points out that it is a mistake to assume that the Swedes have policies towards the poor which are unambiguously liberal, permissive and tolerant. Though the welfare state has broad support, it is very much the creation of a powerful and disciplined trade union movement. Thus the strong tradition of state intervention into families, derived from the Temperance movement, is as much a matter of 'socialist discipline' as 'capitalist oppression', and an insistence on the individual's responsibility to the state as well as vice versa.

Gould describes a network of officially licensed volunteers who are explicitly used as a form of social control. These *övervakare* compulsorily supervise families who have failed to heed, first advice, then orders from the social services to cease certain behaviour. If compulsory supervision fails, the children are taken into public care. But families can also be helped by officially approved 'contact persons' who befriend them and may take the children off their hands for a few hours or at weekends. They have no obligation to report back to the social worker or *övervakare* and are paid generous 'expenses'.

Out of Leninism: Voluntary Action in Eastern Europe

In their historically orthodox form, Leninist parties claim a monopoly of the truth, and of all political activity. They are governed internally by the principles of 'democratic centralism', whereby a self-appointed Politburo manipulates all party elections and, after 'open discussion' in the Central Committee, makes binding decisions and sets policy objectives. These are then implemented by the Secretariat through a tripartite system of management through executives of the state, party and security organs.

All appointments are nominated and vetted by higher party organs, the *Nomenclatura* system, which in most cases excludes non-party people from key positions. The mass of the people are thus excluded from political participation. Political control is extended into every facet of civil society so that no autonomous association is permitted, and the key positions in all permitted organisations are filled through the *Nomenclatura* system. Though religious belief is not outlawed, dominance is conferred upon militant atheist propaganda. Religion is seen as an 'atavistic pursuit doomed to irrelevance in an "advanced socialist" state' and put under threat of extinction.[35]

We can distinguish between East Central and Eastern Europe at the time of the revolutions of 1989–90 using the metaphor of civil society as a fish soup.[36] In Czechoslovakia, East Germany, Hungary and Poland, large fairly intact pieces of civil society, such as religious institutions, private farmers and private businesses, were still floating about. But in the Soviet Union, the soup had been liquidised. But this analogy may be too pessimistic, for it is becoming evident that the Communists' success in suppressing previous civil forms has been overestimated.

In East Central Europe, apart from sporadic revolts, voluntary associations which contested Party control and limited its power were the main means of dissent.[37] Though increasingly involving citizens within groups independent of Party-state control, dissidents attempted to shift the focus of social activity away from the institutions of the communist system towards a more open public domain. Such associations were often sheltered by the churches, who helped to support their internal management, but kept a prudent distance from them to avoid confrontation with the authorities. In periods of relative relaxation these associations sometimes took formal shape, but informal networks for mutual support, mutual help, and the exchange of independent ideas proved more difficult for governments to suppress than large structured organisations. These networks were able to vigorously counter the communist process of mutual mistrust, social division and manipulation and invoked a spirit of solidarity to pierce the barrier of widespread popular fear.

Independent labour unions involved workers in tangible objectives instead of Utopian ones. Groups of intellectuals provided 'flying universities' with non-Party lectures and discussions, financed through illegal publishing. Authentic peace movements developed.

Whilst voluntary action in the social welfare field did not play the major part in these movements, many initiatives took place which were difficult for the Party to combat without putting itself in a bad light, though their operations revealed the extent of the Communists' failure to alleviate poverty. Caritas and the German Protestant welfare association (Diakonisches Werke) operated in East Germany on funds supplied by the West German churches and were tolerated by the Party partly because they provided foreign exchange. Caritas was banned in Poland, but a parallel organisation carried out the same functions largely with Western funds and volunteer help. Its Welfare Solidarity association dispensed medical supplies to needy families. Lay initiatives took place in Hungary and Czechoslovakia.

When Communist rule ended in East Central Europe, the field of voluntary action was faced with problems over its unclear legal status and an archaic tax system offering no concessions. In Hungary, Party bureaucrats transferred state property to 'trusts', appointing themselves directors. More long-term difficulties include general shortage of funds, a weak private enterprise sector able to provide few donations, shortage of management skills and experience, lack of basic equipment, such as computers and photocopiers, and the general preoccupation with basic subsistence.

In the USSR, the Communist system provided outlets for volunteering at the workplace, administered by the official trade unions. The work collective annually elected social insurance delegates, mostly women, whose tasks were to give social assistance to those in need, those who were sick and needed special diet or resort passes, and children who needed day nurseries, summer camps or sanatoria, to monitor health and safety in the workplace and keep abreast of pension and social insurance legislation. In addition to the delegates' paid job, these were formidable tasks.[38]

The *subbotnik* system encouraged individuals to donate a day's paid labour to a state organisation dealing with children, handicapped, or elderly people. Wages which the individual 'would have earned' were also supposed to be credited to the organisation. Involvement in *subbotnik* work was an essential item for the *curriculum vitae* of any ambitious person.

These kinds of voluntary work have probably declined since the trade unions through which they were arranged have partially ceased to function. The Soviets showed less interest in stimulating financial philanthropy, though the Soviet Peace Fund, to which a large proportion of Church collections are diverted, exists to purchase military equipment for Soviet defence.

Unlike East Central Europe or even the Baltics, dissidents cannot look to the Church to protect them. It was actively persecuted until very recently, and the present policy of 'dialogue' can be attributed to a desire to enlist the sympathies of believers on the side of *perestroika* (re-structuring) rather than a lessening of official hostility. At the celebrations of the millenium of Christianity in Russia in 1988, the Church was still prohibited from collecting money for any charity apart from Soviet ones like the Peace Fund, or doing charitable work. The chairman of the State Council for Religious Affairs, Karchev, remarked in a private speech at the Higher Party School that it would put communists in a bad light, 'both morally and politically, to allow believers to carry bedpans'.[39]

'Encouraging citizens to undertake organised initiatives to improve their lot and that of their neighbours outside of the context of the Party and state is no less than revolutionary in this society'.[40] A permit is needed to form an association, and activity in an unrecognised association is dangerous. There is a tendency for authorisations previously granted to be reversed, a discrepancy often exists between the publicly announced and the actual policy towards the associations, and they are unable to own property. For any action, 'permission' must be sought from the party hierarchy. For example, until recently no priest could visit a 'seriously ill' parishioner in a hospital, prison, old persons' home, or other institution without 'permission', which was routinely refused, depriving many of the last rites.[41] A priest continues to need permission to visit a parishioner who is not 'seriously ill'. Actions in associations with others usually require 'permission' from a much higher Party level and even when granted they may, in practice, be denied by lower-level officials. In

1990 most welfare initiatives were linked to new 'co-operative' business ventures,[42] but these have subsequently found themselves in difficulty because of changes in economic policy.

At the time of going to press (September 1991), a coup by senior members of the Soviet Communist Party security apparatus and armed forces in favour of a return to Leninist principles has failed. Devolution of power from the Union to the governments of its constituent republics appears to be under way. But the extent to which the process will disturb existing structures or affect voluntary action in each constituent republic is not yet clear.

Conclusion

Voluntary action has played a useful part in developing a democratic attitude of mind in Western Europe, providing a bridge between merely verbal protest and constructive participation and action within a democratic framework. In East Central Europe voluntary action has played a major role in liberating societies from communism and this could still prove to be the case in the Soviet Union.

In the West, the 'contract culture' may encourage governments to try to use voluntary action in a utilitarian way to the detriment of political participation and consciousness-raising activities. Remembering always that it is the values that it embodies which are the foundations of its strength, voluntary action will doubtless develop new initiatives to contest such restrictions.

CHAPTER 4

WHAT WE KNOW ABOUT VOLUNTEERING: INFORMATION FROM THE SURVEYS

Justin Davis Smith

Introduction: the Problems of Measurement

We are unable to say with any degree of certainty how many people are involved in voluntary activities in Great Britain at the present time. We are even less confident of our ability to trace trends in volunteering over a period of time, but this is not due to the lack of information. There have been no fewer than eight separate attempts to measure the extent of volunteering in Britain over the last 15 years: a National Opinion Poll (NOP) survey for the Wolfenden Committee enquiry into the voluntary sector in 1976; a survey by Social and Community Planning Research (SCPR) for The Volunteer Centre in 1981; the General Household Survey (GHS) of 1981 and 1987; a household survey by the Charities Aid Foundation (CAF) in 1985/86, 1987 and 1988/89; and a MORI survey for The Volunteer Centre UK in 1990.[1]

The main stumbling block to precise measurement is the lack of comparability between the surveys.[2] Different surveys have used different methodologies for measuring volunteering and different definitions of voluntary activity. Some surveys have used a random probability sample; some a quota sample. Some surveys have defined volunteering narrowly as activities undertaken within an organisational framework (or within a registered charity), while others have included informal neighbourhood care within the definition of volunteering. Some surveys have included self-help within the

definition; others have excluded it. The same is true of political and
trade union activity, which some surveys have counted as volunteering and some have not. Some surveys have measured levels of
volunteering amongst all adults in the population aged 16 and over.
Others have restricted measurement to those in the 18 and above age
brackets.

The lack of a common methodology and definition of volunteering
has given rise to widely fluctuating results. For example, the two
surveys carried out in 1981 came up with major variations in
estimates of the level of volunteering. The survey for The Volunteer
Centre by SCPR found that 44 per cent of the adult population had
taken part in voluntary activities during the previous year, whereas
the 1981 General Household Survey put the figure much lower at 23
per cent.[3] While it is not possible to give precise figures of numbers of
volunteers and trends in volunteering, some general conclusions can
be drawn from the surveys about the extent and nature of
volunteering in Britain.

Table 4.1   *The extent of volunteering in Britain*

Survey	Percentage of adult population involved in voluntary activities		
	In past year	In past month	In past week
1976 (NOP)	16	—	9
1981 (Volunteer Centre)	44	27	18
1981 (GHS)	23	15	—
1985/86 (CAF)	—	27	—
1987 (GHS)	23	15	—
1987 (CAF)	—	44	—
1988/89 (CAF)	—	30	—
1990 (MORI)	39	22	—

How Much Volunteering?

With regard to the extent of volunteering in Britain, the surveys tell us
that:

● A substantial proportion of adults in Britain take part in at least
   one voluntary activity during the year. As table 4.1 shows,
   estimates range from about one-fifth of the population (General
   Household Surveys) to almost one-half (1981 Volunteer Centre

Survey). The most recent MORI Survey of 1990 puts the figure at 39 per cent.

- A much smaller proportion of the population volunteers on a regular basis. The 1976 NOP Survey found that 9 per cent of adults had volunteered in the previous week. The 1981 Volunteer Centre Survey found that 27 per cent of people over 18 had volunteered during the previous month, and 18 per cent during the previous week. The 1987 General Household Survey found that 15 per cent of people over 16 had volunteered in the previous month, while the 1990 MORI Survey found a monthly figure of 22 per cent.

- The average time spent on volunteering by adults in Britain works out at less than 5 hours a month. The 1981 Volunteer Centre Survey gave a figure of 1.1 hours a week. The 1987 Charities Aid Foundation Survey found that people volunteered on average for just over 5 hours a month, while the 1988/89 Survey put the monthly average at just over 3 hours.

- The average figure, however, masks large differences in rates of participation. The 1987 General Household Survey found that of the 15 per cent who had volunteered in the previous month, 20 per cent had spent less than 4 hours on volunteering but 7 per cent had spent more than 40 hours. The 1988/89 Charities Aid Foundation Survey found that 16 per cent of volunteers had given less than 5 hours a month, but 2 per cent had given more than 30 hours and a small number had volunteered for as much as 100 hours in the previous month.

- Children under 16 are involved in voluntary activities to a significant degree. The Charities Aid Foundation Surveys alone provide information on children's volunteering. The 1985/86 Survey found that 26 per cent of children aged 10–16 gave some time to volunteering in the last month, at an average of about 4 hours a volunteer, and that 10 per cent of children under 10 had volunteered, at an average of just over 2 hours a month. The 1987 Survey put the figures considerably higher at 42 per cent for the 10–16-year-olds and 25 per cent for the under 10s.

Who Volunteers?

The surveys provide information on the profile of volunteers in Britain:

- Women are more likely to volunteer than men. The 1981 Volunteer Centre Survey found that 52 per cent of current regular volunteers were female. The 1981 General Household Survey found that 24 per cent of women took part in voluntary activities compared with 21 per cent of men, although in the 20–24 age band, and among the over 75s, men were more active. Similar figures were found in the 1987 General Household Survey. The 1990 MORI Survey found that 37 per cent of women and 34 per cent of men were regularly involved in volunteering.
- The optimum age range for volunteering is 35–44, with less younger people and less older people engaged in such activities. The 1981 Volunteer Centre Survey found the highest rates of activity in the 35–44 age band. The 1981 and 1987 General Household Surveys also found the optimum age range for volunteers to be 35–44, with the lowest rates of activity in the 20–24 and 60 plus age brackets. The 1985/86 Charities Aid Foundation Survey found that 40 per cent of regular volunteers were aged 35–44, while the most recent 1990 MORI Survey showed that 42 per cent of regular volunteers were in this age band. However, while older people are less likely to volunteer than people in the middle age ranges, the surveys show that older volunteers give more time to voluntary activities (1987 General Household Survey; 1987 CAF Survey).
- There is a clear link between voluntary activity and socio-economic class, with the higher socio-economic groups showing the highest rates of participation. The 1976 National Opinion Poll Survey found that professional people were three times as likely to volunteer as semi-skilled or manual workers. The 1981 Volunteer Centre Survey found that unskilled manual workers made up only 2 per cent of regular volunteers, compared with 31 per cent for skilled manual workers and 49 per cent for non-manual workers. The 1990 MORI Survey reveals that 60 per cent of regular volunteers were from social groups AB, as compared with only 22 per cent from social groups DE.
- There is a similar relationship in the surveys between the proportion of people doing voluntary activities and other variables associated with socio-economic position, such as educational qualifications and the age of finishing full-time education. The 1987 General Household Survey found that 48 per cent of people with degree-level qualifications had volunteered, compared with 29 per cent with GCE 'A' or 'O' levels and 16 per cent with no qualifications.

- Volunteering is unevenly distributed throughout Britain, perhaps as a consequence of the link with socio-economic class, with the highest participation rates being found in the more prosperous South of England. The 1987 General Household Survey found the South-East of England, outside of London, with the largest proportion of residents (29 per cent) doing volunteering, with the North of England having the lowest rate at 19 per cent. The participation rates in Scotland and Wales were 21 per cent and 20 per cent respectively. The 1990 MORI Survey found that 42 per cent of regular volunteers lived in the South, compared with 34 per cent in the Midlands and 29 per cent in the North.
- People in paid work are more likely to volunteer than people not in paid work. The 1987 General Household Survey found that 63 per cent of all volunteers were working: 45 per cent of them full time, 18 per cent part time. Thirty-seven per cent were outside the paid labour market. The pattern is the same for both men and women, though the proportions differ. The 1987 Survey found that 71 per cent of all men volunteers were in full-time paid work; 6 per cent were in part-time work and 23 per cent were outside the labour market. For women, 53 per cent of volunteers were in paid work, but the majority (28 per cent) were in part-time occupation. Forty-seven per cent of women volunteers were outside the paid labour market.
- People who are unemployed are less likely to volunteer than those in paid work. The 1981 Volunteer Centre Survey found that unemployed people accounted for only 3 per cent of regular volunteers, while a study carried out for the Policy Studies Institute in 1983 found that only 9 per cent of unemployed people took part in voluntary activities, with a majority of these being involved for less than 5 hours a week.[4] The 1987 General Household Survey found that 16 per cent of unemployed people volunteered, compared with 23 per cent of the population as a whole, although for men the figure was only 12 per cent.
- People's propensity to volunteer increases with their income. The 1987 General Household Survey reported that a half of those people with a gross weekly income of more than £450 had volunteered, compared with fewer than a quarter of people with an income of £200 a week or less.
- Black people are under-represented as volunteers. The 1981 Volunteer Centre Survey revealed that 45 per cent of white people were engaged in voluntary activities, compared with 20 per cent of black people, although the small size of the sample of black people

means that the figures have to be treated with caution. The same goes for the 1987 General Household Survey which found that 24 per cent of white people had volunteered in the last 12 months, compared with 19 per cent of West Indian/African people, and only 10 per cent of Indian/Pakistani and Bangladeshi people. Similarly, the 1990 MORI Survey shows black under-representation in voluntary activities, albeit again on low base sizes. These figures are, however, consistent with studies in other countries. A Gallup Poll in the United States in 1985 found that 49 per cent of the white population took part in voluntary activities compared with 38 per cent of the black population, and a 1989 survey by the United States Bureau of Labor Statistics found participation rates of 22 per cent for whites, 12 per cent for blacks, and 9.5 per cent for Hispanics.[5]

- Married people are more likely to volunteer than single people. The 1981 General Household Survey found that 24 per cent of married people took part in voluntary activities, compared with 20 per cent of single people. Similar proportions of married men and women were found to volunteer, but single women were more likely to do so than single men. The 1981 Volunteer Centre Survey showed that 70 per cent of regular volunteers were married, with single people making up only 18 per cent of the total. Widowed and divorced persons made up the remaining 12 per cent. The surveys show that men and women with dependent children are more likely to volunteer than those without. The 1987 General Household Survey reported that 29 per cent of adults with at least one dependent child under 16 had done voluntary work, compared with 20 per cent of adults with no dependent children.

What Volunteers Do

The surveys provide information on the types of activities volunteers are engaged in:

- The most common voluntary activity for both men and women is raising or handling money. The 1976 NOP Survey found that 43 per cent of volunteers were involved in fundraising. The 1981 General Household Survey put the figure at 41 per cent, while the 1981 Volunteer Centre Survey recorded that 68 per cent of volunteers were active in raising or handling money (30 per cent of the entire adult population). The 1987 General Household Survey showed that a massive 75 per cent of volunteers were involved in this field of activity.

- Serving on a committee is another common voluntary activity. The 1976 NOP Survey found 35 per cent of volunteers active in this area, a figure very close to the 36 per cent found in the 1981 Volunteer Centre Survey. The 1990 MORI Survey found that 20 per cent of the adult population had served on a committee in a voluntary capacity.

- Many volunteers are involved in organising or helping with activities or events. The 1976 NOP Survey revealed that 36 per cent of volunteers were so involved, and the 1981 Volunteer Centre Survey found that 54 per cent of volunteers were active in this field. The 1987 General Household Survey put the figure at 47 per cent.

- Secretarial and administrative work involves a significant number of volunteers. The 1976 NOP Survey found 15 per cent of volunteers engaged in this kind of work. The 1987 General Household Survey found that 19 per cent of volunteers were involved in administration of one kind or another, 3 per cent lower than the figure in the 1981 Volunteer Centre Survey.

- Many volunteers are involved in providing transport. The 1976 NOP Survey revealed that 18 per cent of volunteers were active in this area, and the 1981 Volunteer Centre Survey put the figure even higher at 24 per cent.

- Volunteers play an important role in direct service provision. The 1981 Volunteer Centre Survey reported that 25 per cent of volunteers were involved in providing a direct service in the community – a figure which is consistent with the 1987 General Household Survey. The 1990 MORI Survey records that 15 per cent of the population had taken part in providing a direct service in the community on a voluntary basis.

- Representation or advocacy involves 15 per cent of all volunteers, according to the 1981 Volunteer Centre Survey. The 1990 MORI Survey puts the figure at 2 per cent of the adult population.

- Visiting people in institutions involves 11 per cent of volunteers, according to the 1987 General Household Survey. The 1981 Volunteer Centre Survey found that 19 per cent of volunteers were active in visiting or counselling.

Differences in Type of Voluntary Activity by Gender

The surveys show that fundraising is the most common activity for all volunteers. However, differences are revealed in the type of activities undertaken by men and women:

- More women than men are involved in fundraising activities. The 1987 Charities Aid Foundation Survey found that 27 per cent of women and 10 per cent of men had taken part in organising and running a stall at a jumble sale over the last three months; that 23 per cent of women and 13 per cent of men had sold raffle tickets for an organisation; and that 14 per cent of women and only 2 per cent of men had made things, such as cakes and knitted items, to sell for charity. The 1987 General Household Survey reported that 83 per cent of women volunteers were involved in raising and collecting money, compared with 75 per cent of men.
- More men than women serve on committees. The 1987 General Household Survey found that 42 per cent of men volunteers acted as committee members, compared with 32 per cent of women.
- Women are more likely than men to care for the elderly and to undertake visiting and befriending activities. The 1990 MORI Survey found that 48 per cent of women volunteered in 'helping the elderly', compared with 36 per cent of men.
- Men are more likely than women to be involved in advice-giving activities. The 1987 General Household Survey found that 13 per cent of men volunteers and only 6 per cent of women volunteers were involved in advice work. Similarly, 19 per cent of men volunteers and 13 per cent of women volunteers were involved in teaching or training activities.

Differences in Type of Voluntary Activity by Age

The surveys show some variations in the type of voluntary activities undertaken by different age groups:

- More younger than older people take part in sponsored events (1987 Charities Aid Foundation Survey).
- Younger people tend not to serve on committees or get involved in advice work (1987 General Household Survey).
- More older than younger people help at jumble sales. The 1987 Charities Aid Foundation Survey found that 25 per cent of people

over 65 but only 9 per cent of people under 25 helped to organise or run a jumble sale.

• Older volunteers are more likely than younger volunteers to visit people in institutions, such as old people's homes, prisons, or hospitals. The 1987 General Household Survey found that 17 per cent of volunteers in the 60–69 age group and 19 per cent of volunteers over 70 had been involved in visiting activities, compared with only 6 per cent of volunteers in the 35–44 age group and 9 per cent in the 20–24 age bracket. The 1988/89 Charities Aid Foundation Survey found that retired people were particularly active in visiting the sick.

Differences in Type of Voluntary Activity by Class

The surveys show significant differences in voluntary activities according to socio-economic group:

• Serving on committees tends to be the preserve of people from higher socio-economic groups. The 1987 Charities Aid Foundation Survey found that 19 per cent of people from professional and managerial occupations served on committees, compared with only 5 per cent of unskilled manual workers. The 1987 General Household Survey found that over half (52 per cent) of volunteers from professional occupations had served on a committee, whereas less than a quarter (22 per cent) of volunteers from unskilled manual occupations had done so.

• There is a similar pattern with advice work. The 1987 General Household Survey found that 16 per cent of 'professional' volunteers had given advice, compared with 5 per cent of unskilled manual volunteers. The same pattern holds true for teaching and training activities (1987 General Household Survey).

• People from lower socio-economic groups give more help of a practical nature. The 1987 General Household Survey found that 35 per cent of volunteers from the unskilled manual occupation group were involved in such practical activities as transporting, repair work, domestic help and gardening, compared with 23 per cent from the professional group.

Areas of Voluntary Activity

In addition to information on type of activity, the surveys shed light on the fields of activity which volunteers are involved in:

- Up to a third of volunteers are involved in educational activities. The 1981 Volunteer Centre Survey showed that 30 per cent of volunteers were active in this field. The 1990 MORI Survey puts the figure at 33 per cent.

According to the 1981 Volunteer Centre Survey:

- 30 per cent of volunteers are involved in sport or hobby activities.
- 25 per cent of volunteers are involved in welfare or health activities.
- 25 per cent of volunteers are involved with youth work.
- 23 per cent of volunteers are involved in church or religious-based activities.
- 18 per cent of volunteers are involved with community or citizenship activities.
- 11 per cent of volunteers work with the elderly.
- 4 per cent of volunteers are involved in environmental activities.
- 4 per cent of volunteers are involved in political activities.

Trends in Volunteering

There has been much discussion in recent years over whether or not volunteering has declined over the last decade. Some commentators have spoken of a crisis in the recruitment of volunteers. As already noted, the surveys of volunteering are not comparable, so we are unable to trace trends in volunteering with any degree of confidence. Nevertheless, some tentative conclusions can be drawn about the movement of volunteering during the 1980s.

- The surveys offer conflicting evidence on the recruitment crisis. The surveys conducted over several years by the Charities Aid Foundation offer some support to the view that volunteering has declined. The 1987 Survey, for example, found that the average number of hours volunteered by all adults was just over 5. In comparison, the 1988/89 Survey found the average to be 3 hours 20 minutes. On the other hand, the two General Household Surveys – of 1981 and 1987 – came up with an identical figure for the percentage of the adult population involved in volunteering,

23 per cent, even though different definitions of volunteering were used.

- Whilst the total number of people involved in volunteering may have remained constant during the 1980s, there appears to have been an increase in activity in the environmental field. The 1981 Volunteer Centre Survey found 4 per cent of volunteers engaged in environmental activities. In contrast, the 1990 MORI Survey put the figure at 11 per cent.

- The opposite appears to be true of volunteering through the church or other religious institution. The 1981 Volunteer Centre Survey found that 23 per cent of volunteers were involved in religious activities. The 1990 MORI Survey found only 14 per cent of volunteers involved in this area.

Reasons for Volunteering

The surveys provide some information on the reasons why people volunteer.

- Altruism is an important motivation to volunteer. The 1988/89 Charities Aid Foundation Survey found that altruism was the motivating factor for almost 50 per cent of volunteers, although the 1981 Volunteer Centre Survey put the figure much lower at 10 per cent.

- Having a personal interest in an activity is another important motivation. The 1981 Volunteer Centre Survey reported that more than a third of volunteers got involved for this reason. The 1988/89 Charities Aid Foundation Survey put the figure at 24 per cent.

- Many volunteers get involved in response to a direct request for assistance. The 1981 Volunteer Centre Survey cited this as the 'motivating' factor for 11 per cent of volunteers.

- Religious concerns motivate 10 per cent of volunteers, according to the 1981 Volunteer Centre Survey.

- Filling in spare time is given as the main reason for volunteering by 5 per cent of respondents in the 1981 Volunteer Centre Survey, and by 8 per cent in the 1988/89 Charities Aid Foundation Survey.

- Getting work experience is the motivating factor for 2 per cent of volunteers, according to the 1988/89 Charities Aid Foundation Survey.

A Qualitative Study of Motivations

A statistical analysis of why people volunteer is of limited value, as the above figures show. One of the drawbacks to a survey-based approach to motivation is that it may lead to an overstatement of the importance of altruism as a motivating factor. Confronted with a check-list of reasons for volunteering, it is possible that people will choose the one most socially acceptable, that is wanting to help others. In an attempt to overcome this problem, in 1990 The Volunteer Centre UK commissioned Social and Community Planning Research (SCPR) to carry out a qualitative study of people's motivations to volunteer.[6] The study, based on a series of group discussions with volunteers and non-volunteers from a range of different socio-economic backgrounds, provides an insight into why people take up voluntary activities, and why people choose not to volunteer. The study is a useful addition to the surveys, and is worth summarising briefly.

Why People Volunteer

As table 4.2 shows, the SCPR study, in line with the surveys, found that people volunteered for a variety of reasons. Some volunteered for altruistic reasons; others because they had a particular interest which they wanted to pursue or because they wanted to learn new skills. Some people got involved in volunteering through their children; others through their paid work. Many people, however, got involved in volunteering almost by accident. For many people, volunteering was not a premeditated action. Rather they had taken it up on the spur of the moment in response to a direct request for help from a friend or relative. One volunteer in the study summed it up thus: 'Well I was asked by somebody that goes if I'd like to do it and I said, "yes I will." ' The spur-of-the-moment nature of much voluntary activity is borne out by the statistics. The 1981 Volunteer Centre Survey found that 35 per cent of volunteers got involved through a relative and a further 22 per cent through a friend or acquaintance. The 1990 MORI Survey found that two-thirds of volunteers were recruited through a friend or relative.

Table 4.2 *Why volunteer?: initial motivations, as described by volunteers*

'Because I was asked'
(Asked directly, or pressure brought to bear)
- through one's children/children's activities
  (eg parents' committee)
- through friends, neighbours, or others in need
- through existing association with an organisation
  (eg playgroups)
- for some, through having a particular skill to offer

'I had time on my hands'
(Particularly if retired, or not working full-time)
- 'to give me something to do'
- to stave off boredom
- to provide a structure to the day

To continue an existing association
Either:
- transition from 'member' to 'leader' (eg youth club, Guides)
'to give something back'
- as a way of continuing an enjoyable activity
Or:
- always been a volunteer

Personal circumstance or other link with need
- illness/disability
- having (or knowing) a disabled child

A chance to make a contribution or 'pay back'
- to a particular organisation
- in the wider sense, to society

General philosophy/beliefs
- one 'ought' to help; social conscience
- always been a volunteer; a tradition of volunteering

'It sounded/seemed interesting'
- saw others enjoying it
- saw an advert

Source: SCPR, *On Volunteering: A Qualitative Study of Images, Motivations and Experiences* (The Volunteer Centre UK, 1990).

Why People Do Not Volunteer

As table 4.3 shows, the study found that some people did not volunteer because they had not got the time, or because they chose to spend their leisure time doing something else. Others did not volunteer because they felt that they would become over-committed. Some people did not volunteer because of the financial costs involved, in terms of travel and other out-of-pocket expenses. The study found that some women were put off volunteering because they were afraid to go out at night. Others did not get involved because they equated volunteering exclusively with fundraising and found asking people for money distasteful. For some people, volunteering did not have any appeal. As one interviewee explained: 'Volunteering is like a hobby and I choose my hobbies because they interest me, and I choose not to volunteer because it doesn't interest me.' For many people, however, the reason for not volunteering was very simple: they had never been asked. One non-volunteer said: 'Well, nobody ever asked me. If somebody approached me . . . then I would.'

Table 4.3   *Why not volunteer? The non-volunteers' view*

'You just don't seem to find the time'
- too busy
- difficult to fit around work
- family commitments
- clashes with leisure activities
- inconvenient

Potential disadvantages
- It might cost me money
- It might mean having to go out at night
- It might mean having to raise money/ask people for money
  ('I'd be embarrassed')
- It might mean getting over-involved

Suspicion
- In relation to fundraising: 'Where is the money going?'
- Possible exploitation of volunteers by their organisations

'I'm not that sort of person'
- 'I'm young and single, it hasn't appealed so far'
- You have to 'see a need'/'be touched by something'
- Active decision to do other things

'Well, nobody's ever asked me'

Source: SCPR, *On Volunteering.*

Why People Stop Volunteering

Why people stop volunteering is as of much interest as non-participation. The SCPR study suggests a number of reasons why volunteers drop out (see table 4.4). The study found that some people left volunteering because of changes in their personal circumstances. For example, they moved house, changed jobs, or started a family.

Others, however, dropped out of volunteering because they had become over-committed: too much was asked of them by the organisation. As one interviewee put it: 'Well, it was half a day a week, then a day a week, then two days a week, then three days a week, then going out Sundays and going out night times, until it got nearly a full-time job.' Some people had stopped volunteering because of organisational problems. Some complained of the lack of professionalism of voluntary groups; others of the lack of training and support they were given for the tasks they were asked to do. For some people, volunteering had lost its appeal. Others had given up because they did not feel that their contribution to the organisation was being recognised. The consequences of the lack of organisation for the retention of volunteers is brought out in the surveys. The 1981 Volunteer Centre Survey found that one in four volunteers felt that their organisation could be better managed, and one in six required additional back-up and support.

Table 4.4 *Why do people stop being a volunteer?: ex-volunteers' views*

Personal reasons
- lose contact through moving house/changing job
- no longer relevant

Over-commitment
- become too involved
- inflexibility of involvement where personal circumstances change, eg greater responsibility at work

Disenchantment with volunteering
- volunteering loses its appeal

Source: SCPR, *On Volunteering*.

International Comparisons

Attempts to measure volunteering have not been restricted to Britain. Surveys have been carried out in a number of countries of mainland Europe and in North America. Table 4.5 summarises the findings of some of the most recent of these surveys.[7]

As with the various British surveys, these surveys are not comparable (with the exception perhaps of the American ones), because of the use of different methodologies and different definitions of volunteering. However, as with the British surveys, a number of common themes do emerge:

- Women are more likely to volunteer than men. The 1987 Canadian Survey found that 55 per cent of formal volunteers were women, compared with 45 per cent of men. The 1990 Survey in the United States revealed that 52 per cent of men volunteered, compared with 56 per cent of women. In Denmark, however, the pattern is reversed. The 1986 Survey showed that men comprised 56 per cent of regular volunteers and women 44 per cent.
- Most volunteers are in the middle age groups. The 1990 United States Survey found most volunteers to be between the ages of 25 and 44, with a decline in participation after 55. In the 1987 Canadian Survey and the 1986 Dutch Survey the peak age for volunteering was identified as 35–44. In Denmark the 1986 Survey found that a third of all volunteers were in the age range 35–44.
- People from higher socio-economic groups are most likely to volunteer. The 1987 Canadian Survey found that 18 per cent of people with a household income of less than $10,000 volunteered, compared with 39 per cent of those with an income of more than $60,000. Similar findings emerge from the surveys in the United States, the Netherlands and Denmark.
- Most volunteers are married. The 1990 United States Survey revealed that 59 per cent of married people volunteered, compared with 44 per cent of single people. The same pattern was reported in the surveys from Canada and Denmark.

Table 4.5 *The extent of volunteering in North America and mainland Europe*

Country	Year of survey	Percentage of adult population involved in voluntary activity
Belgium	1980	15
Canada	1987	27 (formal) 70 (informal)
Demark	1986	24
France	1981	32*
Netherlands	1986	45
USA	1985	48
USA	1987	45
USA	1988	42
USA	1990	54

* This study looked at membership of voluntary organisations.

Conclusion

What can we conclude about volunteering in Britain (and in other countries) from the surveys? First, that volunteering is an activity undertaken by a significant proportion of the population – anything from a quarter to one half of the adult population, although much of this activity is on a one-off basis; the number of regular 'active' volunteers being much smaller. Second, we can conclude that some people are more likely to be involved in voluntary activities than others. The surveys tell us that volunteers are likely to be in paid work, especially in managerial positions and professional occupations; to be educated to further or higher educational level; to be married and have children; to be aged 35–44; and to be white. However, before we conclude that volunteering is the preserve of the white middle classes, let us sound a couple of notes of caution.

We should perhaps guard against over-stressing the connection between volunteering and class. There is some evidence to suggest that the findings in the surveys are being skewed by the definitions of volunteering used. For example, a survey carried out by MORI for the *Reader's Digest* magazine in 1989, while finding that volunteers were most likely to come from higher socio-economic groups, revealed that people caring for elderly neighbours in an informal capacity were more likely to come from lower socio-economic groups.[8] This suggests one of two things. Either the surveys of volunteering are measuring only formal, organised activity and that such activity is biased towards the middle classes, or that 'volunteering' as a term has middle-class associations. The consequence of this could be that people from lower socio-economic groups are failing to recognise their activities in the community as volunteering, seeing them instead as examples of informal caring and neighbourliness. A survey which adopts a broad definition of volunteering to embrace informal neighbourhood activity as well as organised, formal activity, and which makes allowances for possible under-recording due to difficulties in terminology, might well find a much reduced link between volunteering and social class. There is evidence, however, that the link is unlikely to disappear altogether.

As with the figures on class, the figures on race need to be treated carefully. It would be wrong to conclude from the surveys that black people do not volunteer. A study of black volunteering in London by the Black Perspectives in Volunteering Group and ADVANCE in 1988 found evidence of extensive voluntary activity within the black community, particularly of the mutual-aid and self-help type.[9] What appears to be happening is that such activity is not being recorded in the statistics, either because self-help is being overlooked by the surveys or because black people do not recognise it as volunteering. In this sense, volunteering may not only be a class-based concept but a cultural one as well.

PART TWO

CURRENT ISSUES

CHAPTER 5

ORGANISING AND MANAGING VOLUNTEERS

Rodney Hedley

Introduction

The most recent estimates of the numbers of volunteers show that, at any one time, 39 per cent of the adult population take part in voluntary activity.[1] The range of tasks in which volunteers are involved varies enormously – from door-to-door canvassing for political parties, to shaking tins on flag days; from chairing committees, to dressing up as clowns for local playgroups; from representing social security claimants in appeal tribunals, to sticking up posters to advertise jumble sales; from saving lives in the North Sea, to counselling those who experience trauma following a disaster such as Zeebrugge. The time involvement and frequency of volunteering varies enormously – survey data from 1981 shows that 66 per cent of all volunteers give at least three hours a week, and 14 per cent engage in voluntary activity for over 11 hours a week. While half of those who volunteer involve themselves in one agency only, a quarter of volunteers work for two agencies, and 10 per cent for three or more agencies.[2]

The responsibilities undertaken by volunteers are large and varied. Some would argue that Britain's voluntary sector is voluntary only by virtue of its volunteer management committees who receive no financial reward or profit. In recent years the trend has been for many voluntary organisations, especially in the welfare field, to have a majority of their management committees made up of representatives from *paid staff* from other voluntary bodies or statutory agencies. While these people receive no direct financial reward for their participation, they are paid by their host organisation to attend, and may act on their host's behalf. Whether a management committee regularly meets in the daytime or night time is a good test of how 'voluntary' it is: daytime meetings are preferred by paid staff. These volunteers oversaw the dispersal of £15 billion pounds of resources in 1989, equivalent to 4 per cent of gross domestic product, and manage an industry that employs around 300,000 people and is as big as the car industry.[3] Taking the local authority sector, 8,500 volunteer councillors are responsible for resources of £40 billion and are responsible for a paid staff of around 600,000.[4] Further, the Centre for Policy Studies has estimated that: 'When the unpaid efforts of charity volunteers are added to the monetary contributions made to the sector as a whole, the cost of replacing the work of the voluntary sector would be well in excess of £20 billion – or some 12p or 13p on the basic rate of income tax.'[5]

So what about the organisation and management of these vast numbers of people? We have to consider the range of voluntary activity. Let us take a few examples.

Football referees are volunteers. Their training typically takes three years, in which they have to demonstrate commitment, knowledge and skill, as well as keeping physically fit. They also have to show a good mental temperament! They take examinations. Once 'qualified' they are still under strict management and supervision. Indeed, they receive supervision levels which many workers in regular paid jobs would not expect – nor welcome. This supervision does not include the additional verdicts from players, crowds, press, or television. Even at the top of the profession, the financial rewards to referees are at the expenses level – and these people work alongside footballers who earn many thousands of pounds in the same 90 minutes. Thus strict organisation and management are essential to the nature of refereeing – as is its voluntary status. Not to have that tight organisation and control would defeat the purpose of the endeavour.

In contrast to football referees let us consider the work of local councillors. While councillors are accountable to the electorate, their management and organisation go through their party machine. We cannot really think of Ken Livingstone, former leader of the GLC, and a volunteer in that capacity, as being directly supervised in any 'line management' way. But peer pressure is exerted. In the political process, discussion and group decision-making are the keys to volunteer management and organisation. The absence of that discussion and group participation would defeat the purpose of the task.

But let us take another voluntary activity – helping to run a local fete. Here a group of people may decide to share a number of everyday tasks. Anyone attempting to directly supervise the activity is likely to be resented. Indeed, to try and manage such an activity may well defeat its purpose. There will certainly be tensions. The scriptwriters of the *Archers* are certainly aware of this phenomenon and few village events pass without some argument arising between bossy organisers and recalcitrant Ambridge folk – volunteers one and all.

Given this vast range of activities and contexts in which volunteers are involved, a chapter on organising and managing volunteers is over-ambitious. However, in what follows, I do hope to identify and discuss a number of issues and ideas which may be of assistance to those working in this area. So that basic details in the recruitment and deployment of volunteers are not forgotten, at the end of the chapter there is a check list on involving volunteers in the work of an agency.

Motivation for Work

As we go into the 1990s, management is a buzz word. Bookshops are full of glossy paperbacks showing how success can be achieved and how Japanese methods might be applicable to 'your company'. One approach is to treat the organisation and management of volunteers as you would that of paid workers. (You will not, however, find volunteering cited in the indexes of these books.)

Management theorists seem to spend a lot of time on motivation – motivation to work and motivation at the workplace. Motivation is not only seen as the key to better company performance, but also to ensure that workers are content and satisfied.

Management pundits start with the question, why work? Observing our capitalist society evolve, with the mass of people either in employed drudgery or periodically out of work, Karl Marx commented that the only thing that held people to their jobs was the 'cash nexus,' that is, the money wage. For most people, this was at the subsistence level.[6] In the post-industrial world of the 1990s, Britain and other developed nations can take another approach to work. While unemployment and poverty is still endemic, much of the drudgery has gone out of many occupations. Salaries and conditions have improved and most people talk of 'having a career' – work appears to offer more than simply a cash reward.

Looking at how people contemplate paid work, Maslow speculated that people were subject to a 'hierarchy of needs'.[7] He identified needs thus:

- self-actualisation needs
- esteem needs
- belonging needs
- safety needs
- physiological needs

Our minimum needs are physiological – we all need food, warmth and shelter. Maslow argued that once these needs are satisfied – say through earning a minimum money wage – people look to meet the higher needs, such as esteem. Maslow's ideas were developed by Herzberg, who divided the need elements into 'hygiene factors' and 'motivational factors'.[8] Hygiene factors had to be provided at an adequate level for people to perform; *not* providing these factors would mean that people would be demotivated, or would simply not work for the organisation. However, providing more of these hygiene elements would not necessarily increase motivation (if your wages were doubled tomorrow, would you necessarily work harder?). For real motivation, Herzberg returned to Maslow's higher needs, and discussed the need for individuals at work to experience self-fulfilment, creativity, and to have a sense of responsibility.

McGregor had a more robust view regarding management. His XY theory postulated two views of humankind: people need to be pushed and cajoled into work – theory X; or they push themselves – theory Y. Managers have to respond accordingly, either in an authoritarian or participatory manner. Revealingly, McGregor carried out some of his research in school settings.[9]

Reviewing these motivation theories, Handy has devised something called the 'motivation calculus'.[10] This says that individuals will expand energy to fulfil their needs, providing the result of the effort adequately meets those needs. It sounds elementary, but it is a useful tool in understanding how people approach their work – volunteers or employees.

To show how it operates, Handy gives the example of an employee who has a high need for 'power'. If he or she is given a task which may result in promotion, he or she will give more *effort* to it if it is believed that good performance leads to promotion, and that promotion will satisfy the need for power.

Every day we are all making decisions on that basis. Evidence from work settings shows how the calculus appears to operate: people who set themselves targets are not only more committed to them, but actually achieve them; people who achieve their goals, set higher ones; those who fail to meet goals, set lower ones. The crucial point for managers is that individual needs are complex and vary over time.

Motivation for Volunteering?

But let us get back to volunteering. The statistics show that most volunteers are economically secure – there is a middle-class bias – and therefore, in Maslow's terms, their basic needs have been met. As a recent document by ADVANCE puts it:

> With the exception of financial reward, volunteering can provide people with many of the benefits derived from paid work: purposeful, enjoyable activities through which individuals can, for example, make social contacts, develop their skills and competence and grow in confidence and self esteem. It offers the opportunity for people with different talents and abilities to contribute to society, in some cases leading on to their gaining paid employment in a related field.[11]

A recent research report into why people volunteer certainly emphasises the 'higher needs' elements identified by the management theorists.[12] Hence volunteers find the activities in which they are involved pleasurable; they feel they can use skills; they feel that they are making a contribution to society; they enjoy face-to-face work (volunteering is biased towards 'people' activities); and they see volunteering as a way to make friends. Altruism remains important. Indeed, while many agencies promote volunteering in terms of individuals gaining skills and gaining paid employment – the ADVANCE quote above, for example – altruism must not be forgotten. As the research report *Black People and Volunteering* pointed out, 'gaining of new skills is seen as a by-product of volunteering'.[13]

Managing Volunteers: What Volunteers Appear to Want and Expect

In May 1990 the research report *On Volunteering: A Qualitative Research Study of Images, Motivations and Experiences* was published.[14] It was based on group discussions with a mix of 70 past and

present volunteers, and non-volunteers. What did they say which
would help volunteer organisers in their management?

Attracting Volunteers

On attracting volunteers, the respondents felt that the 'image' of
volunteering, and of volunteers, needed overhauling. They felt that
volunteering should be marketed in a professional way, not only to
uplift the image, but to provide more information to would-be
candidates. Too many volunteer recruitment campaigns were
amateurish. They felt that expenses should be paid and, where
necessary, training be given. Having said that, they also felt that the
best way for anyone to get involved in volunteering was to be asked
personally. This echoes the survey findings which show that a third of
volunteers get involved through friends or neighbours, with only 1 or
2 per cent being recruited through radio, press campaigns, or
volunteer bureaux. For the black community, personal contact as a
recruitment method appears to be even more important.

Retaining Volunteers

Getting volunteers is one thing; retaining them is another. Most
volunteers drop out because of changes in personal circumstances.
Whereas paid work determines our life-style (move job, move home);
our life-style determines voluntary activity. However, time commitment is a major issue for volunteers – there seems to be an inevitable
pressure to do more and saying 'no' is difficult:

> 'I started off with just every other Friday, now it's every
> afternoon.'

> 'You have to be very careful that you don't get swept into too
> many things you can't cope with eventually.'

> 'Well people don't take no for an answer, they keep going over
> the years, and it's very difficult to say no.'

A number of ways of managing the time problem were suggested.
To quote the report:

Once a person has expressed an interest in becoming a volunteer, it was considered essential that the type of activities they will be asked to participate in and the level of commitment required are explained in detail. This allows three processes to occur. First it allows the volunteer to get a 'feel' for the organisation and the type of activities in which it is involved. Second it allows volunteers to determine their own levels of commitment. Third the organisation has the opportunity to gauge a person's interest and requirement so that an individual can be matched, where possible, to a particular voluntary activity.

It was also seen as essential to get volunteers involved as soon as possible, but also as gradually as possible – volunteers should not do 'too much too soon'.

Considering the problems over time commitment, it was suggested that organisers of volunteers should maintain contact so that they could be alerted to the changing social, domestic and paid-employment demands on the volunteers.

Perhaps bearing in mind Handy's motivation calculus, it was considered essential to match activities to people's interests and skills, but that this should not be seen as a static process. People's interests change all the time, hence activities would have to change, in many cases making the work more mixed and varied. Training should be encouraged to facilitate this matching, and to achieve better, and more enjoyable, performance.

Appreciation is necessary: the job in itself not being enough. The organiser – or the organisation – has to express a 'thank you' in some form:

'A pat on the back goes down well.'

'Social do's and a Christmas party – just the thing.'

It was also suggested that such appreciation should be expressed more formally in terms of a certificate. This idea was of most interest to younger people in the sample, the rationale behind the suggestion being that the work had not only been done but had been done well.

Provision of expenses was seen as necessary to secure regular commitment and longer-term commitment, especially for those on low incomes.

There were also reflections on management and organisation: 'No one wants to be associated with an organisation that's disorganised; it makes you feel as if no one cares.' The sample of respondents wanted a more 'professional' and 'organised' approach to be taken by the volunteer-using bodies. The views elicited in 1990, cross reference well with the 1981 national survey of volunteering which found that 45 per cent of active volunteers felt that their organisations could be 'better organised, offer better back up, or have a better vision' of where they were going.[15]

Remember this Letter

The letter below sums up the research evidence pretty well. It was published in *Involve Magazine* in 1985, and was written by a group of volunteer organisers putting themselves in the shoes of prospective volunteers.[16]

Dear Organization,
When I begin volunteering, please outline:

- What will I have to do?
- How much time must I give?
- What do I do if something goes wrong?
- What training are you going to give me?
- After I have been volunteering for a while, will you encourage me to take the initiative in suggesting new ways of doing things?
- How will you build up and maintain my skills?
- Is there a support group for volunteers?
- Will you let me know my limitations, and when it is time to ask for help?
- Have you thought of advertising our services/skills more widely?
- If I am given more responsibility within the organisation, how will you support me?
- If I get tired of what I'm doing, will you help me to leave gracefully or give me a new challenge?

Yours voluntarily,

Organisational Perspectives

Let us take a look at how one organisation uses volunteers so that we can examine some of the mangement issues involved. The organisation concerned is a charity which has the prime aim of raising funds to finance education and health projects in a third world country. The charity is relatively new – five years old. It was created when a committed number of activists came together to see whether they could help with the needs of a particular country. It is based in London.

At the beginning, two of the activists ensured that there was a programme of work and a system for carrying it out: sending letters to trusts and individuals for contributions, and arranging fund-raising events. The activists 'brought in anyone who could help out'. The charity became registered,and operated under a trust deed. A management committee was formed. For the first two years all the work was carried out voluntarily. However, such was the organisation's growth that a paid job was identified, and the management committee decided to appoint a co-ordinator. With the aid of a charitable grant, funding was made available and as a result one of the founder volunteer activists who had built up the organisation became the first paid worker.

The organisation has continued to grow. At the present time it has the following personnel: a management committee of 12 members; 2 paid workers, both of whom have a brief for recruiting and organising volunteers; 1 specialist consultant on contract to assist with public relations; 4 office volunteers, who help with the central administration; and a pool of around 25 volunteers to help out with big administration jobs, such as mass mail-outs of appeal letters. Subscribers to the organisation are numbered in their thousands; regular supporters, measured by those who receive newsletters number around 700. One of the workers mapped out the structure of the organisation as shown in table 5.1.

Table 5.1 *The way a volunteer-using organisation is managed*

Organisation function	Personnel
Management committee	12 volunteers
Office administration	2 paid staff, plus 4 office volunteers
Mass mail-outs	25 volunteers
Press/publicity	1 paid consultant
Supporters	700
Subscribers	2,000

How Did People Get Involved in the Organisation?

It is interesting to note how people came into the organisation. Those on the management committee clearly identified with the cause of this third world country, and all had experience of third world issues, at least half the committee being involved in other development agencies (some professionally as paid workers). Constituted as a trust, recruitment to the management committee was by self-selection.

Of the two paid staff, one, as we noted, had been a founder activist; the other one had been recruited through advertisement and open competition. The paid consultant had been recommended by another third world agency. The four office volunteers had been recruited from the local volunteer bureau.

While these office volunteers were sympathetic to the cause of the charity, the cause itself was not the prime reason for their involvement. They had been looking for an activity requiring the use of their office skills, and wanted to volunteer for a socially useful agency which offered a good working environment. They could, in fact, have just as easily worked for another charity.

The office volunteers can be contrasted with the pool of 25 volunteers who help with the monthly mail-out – a two-hour session of collating papers and stuffing envelopes. These were, in the main, supporters of the organisation who had found time to give a little help on a regular basis.

How Are the Volunteers Organised and Managed?

The management committee
The management committee had worked out its division of labour with regard to the staff. Contracts of employment, and terms and conditions of service had been issued to staff. The agency used model documents, as available in the guide *Voluntary But Not Amateur.*[17] Salaries were comparable to other third world charities and tied to national scales for cost-of-living rises.

The trust was the final authority in the management of the agency. The committee entrusted the paid staff to see to the day-to-day work, and for them to initiate and research new ideas. The committee saw itself as being responsible for wider policy matters and for 'networking' with other agencies. The members of the committee only received expenses in special circumstances. While there were honorary officers, very rarely was action taken by the chair. It was commented: 'The management committee secretary takes the minutes; the staff type them.' A seemingly trivial point, but relevant in indicating respective roles.

All management committee meetings were open to both staff and volunteers. The management committee expected the paid staff to manage the volunteers.

The four office volunteers
The office volunteers carried out administration – typing, filing, keeping records, dealing with telephone and postal enquiries. Two volunteers worked two sessions a week; the other two worked one session a week. A division of labour had evolved: one volunteer was responsible for subscriptions; another for the layout of the newsletter; the other two were available for 'bits and pieces'.

All volunteers were offered travel expenses; coffee and tea were freely on tap; and those working over a lunch period were offered a meal allowance. All office volunteers had a job description – a few sentences to describe the duties to be undertaken. All volunteers also received an information sheet setting out how the office was organised, such as details about expenses, the trust and other matters.

Crucial to the employment of the office volunteers was the role of the local volunteer bureau. The agency had informed the bureau of its need for office volunteers with proven office skills. The bureau had the right people available. Because the bureau had time to interview and counsel volunteers, they arrived well briefed. The bureau ensured that the charity had drawn up a job description and person specification (the latter outlining the minimum skills required for the job). The four volunteers still underwent an interview, and a trial period, but the bureau, in effect, had carried out the personnel function of recruitment and selection.

A further consideration was equal opportunities. The charity had a policy on this and, in working for a black third world country, was perhaps proactive in its attitude to race. The bureau, however, in its advertising, recruitment and selection was sensitive to equal opportunity matters. One of the volunteers is black.

So far the volunteer placement system has worked well: volunteers who have left have done so because of changes in their personal circumstances.

The pool of 25 volunteers
The pool of 25 volunteers came from supporters of the charity living

in the Greater London area. These volunteers had responded to requests in the newsletter or, at some time, had responded to advertisements in the *New Statesman and Society's* 'Volunteers' Noticeboard.' These volunteers were initially briefed 'over the telephone' and were just asked to turn up. Expenses for travel were paid. Mail-outs were usually carried out in the early evening. The job was a social task with teams of people chattering, tea and biscuits being served in healthy quantities, and sometimes the session being followed by a drink in the pub afterwards. People who found the work boring simply dropped out. There are no great expectations about the work. However, over a period of three years there still remains a core of very loyal people.

The Management and Organisational Secrets

Things appear to be running smoothly in this charity – too smoothly the reader may comment – but what are the secrets of successful management and organisation?

Firstly, the organisation has a cause which is identifiable and measurable – meeting fund-raising targets. The key to this is that everyone can work towards a common goal and are all pulling together. The fact that they are meeting pressing needs in the third world aids this process – but this is not a factor in itself. (This is not to imply that third world charities have no problems with regard to goal setting, as the case of War on Want illustrated.) All the activists could see what was being achieved and, as the cliché goes, 'success breeds success'. A common problem for many welfare agencies is that they cannot be clear about their goals, and they spend more time and energy on arguing about objectives than planning how to meet the need. This obviously affects motivation, especially of volunteers who often cannot understand what their 'managers' are arguing about.

Secondly, the two workers responsible for the volunteers worked as part of a team. They were physically in the same room as the office volunteers, and worked on the mail-outs, stuffing envelopes with everyone else. Hence they could share the experience, and help adjust and change workloads accordingly. For the office volunteers, a creative division of labour emerged.

Thirdly, the agency had been clear about what it expected from volunteers. Minimum requirements and standards were laid down. The charity had learnt from other volunteer-using agencies, and allowed the volunteer bureau to have a major role in recruitment and selection, also using its expertise in drawing up job descriptions and person specifications.

Fourthly, the organisers ensured that a number of hygiene factors were met – to use the jargon, explained on page 96. With the payment of expenses, an obstacle to volunteering had been removed. However, the organisers were frank in saying that in one particular hygiene factor (almost, but not quite literally) they were lacking. The charity's offices were cramped and dingy and not always conducive to good performance – 'I'm sure we're breaking health and safety rules for staff, let alone for anyone else.' Virtue was made of necessity and the poor office conditions were made a part of the sharing – there was no discrimination between volunteers and staff, they all 'lumped it', and could joke about it. Concern was expressed, however, in that the offices were not suitable for wheelchair access and, as a result, the charity could not fully comply with equal opportunities.

Fifthly, there was the style of the volunteer organisers. What was the magic ingredient? One summed up her approach as follows:

We try to be open for one thing. I don't think there's any secrets. Certainly no 'them and us'. I hope not anyway. We lay down standards which are I think achievable, and we work on problems together, yet for some jobs volunteers do take the initiative. Volunteers must know they can approach us at any time, talk to us about any problem . . . It all boils down to TLC – tender loving care. That doesn't mean we are soft on them, but it means we recognise them as individuals. I suppose this is the real difference between paid members of staff and volunteers. As a volunteer organiser I feel I have to be in some way responsible for the individual – support and supervision are one and the same thing. I have to know the job, and the person in the job. Hence I have to make it my priority to remember Christian names; whether people have been away on holiday; their husbands' names, wives' names, ages of children, and so on. I have to recognise and understand their personal world. With a work colleague you don't feel you have to do that so much. It probably sounds patronising, but it isn't meant to be. I hope it isn't.

In fact the need to recognise the personal needs of volunteers was seen as one of the biggest strains of the job of volunteer organising. This organiser continued: 'I suppose that's the biggest stress factor.

Organising tasks like mail-outs is easy. But remembering 25 individuals' personal circumstances isn't. People say I work for a tiny organisation – they forget how many people I have to sometimes manage. All with a smile!'

But Why Use Volunteers?

But why use volunteers? This was always an issue for the charity – however, it addressed the question differently: what resources do we need to maximise our fund-raising?

The agency had been founded on volunteer labour. As it grew, it was assessed to be more efficient and effective to convert some of the unpaid work into paid work, with a recognition that volunteers should still be used. The agency had grown and was viable because of volunteers. But there were crucial management choices.

On the one hand, it was accepted that *not* to have the skilled office volunteers would mean finding about £10,000 to buy in a worker – or a cutting back on activities. Hence, while the system worked, office volunteers were considered a net gain after allowing for the management and organisation costs in deploying volunteers. Indeed, it had been hoped that a volunteer might carry out some of the press work, but such was the expertise and time commitment needed that no volunteer could be found, and a paid consultant was therefore contracted.

On the other hand, the charity was seriously debating giving its mass mail-out job to a private company. Although this major task appeared to be carried out for free, and while it created 'good will', it was not seen as an effective way of deploying paid workers' time. Put bluntly, volunteers were perceived as a net cost to the agency. Good will could be secured in other ways. The mail-out volunteers had been consulted and, as we might expect, most said that they would be ready to help out in other areas of work when and where necessary. They accepted without rancour that this policy was in the best interests of the charity – and the cause.

We can see how the role of volunteers within the agency changed even in this short history of five years. To quote the organiser:

As we grow, roles are bound to change. We can't be prescriptive about the use of volunteers. We may use more paid staff and more volunteers; we may use more paid staff and less volunteers. Also if we were to contract we may use more volunteers –

possibly at the expense of paid workers if the need arose. In planning change we would always honour procedures and negotiate fully, referring to such things as the Drain Guidelines [see page 117], but the aims of the agency come first. Why exist otherwise?

Volunteer Participation

The decision to stop using volunteers, or paid workers, was a role for the management committee. In this charity, as we have noted, volunteers had the right to attend ordinary meetings and were free to lobby, but there was no constitutional machinery, such as an annual meeting, for volunteers to express their influence on the government of the agency in a formal way. Volunteers were advised that they could join a union, taking advantage of the Manufacturing Science and Finance (MSF) free membership scheme. In many agencies, volunteers perhaps have more apparent power in that they, as members or users, can democratically change government or policy. One of the issues for this charity was that its beneficiaries – or users – were 6,000 miles away.

Organisational Expectations Meet Volunteer Expectations

Can we draw some general lessons from this example? Organisations have their objectives. Volunteers are deployed to secure the achievement of those objectives, but come with a range of expectations – some of which may be in conflict with the aims of the agency. Successful organisation and management is ensuring that both sets of expectations are matched.

Contracts and Bureauracies

We can perhaps understand this in terms of a contract. Handy refers to three types of contract by which individuals attach themselves to organisations. The *coercive contract* is when we have to comply – for example, hospitalisation, some aspects of schooling, and prisons or compulsory community service. In 1989 the Hollywood star, Zsa Zsa Gabor, was sentenced to seven days' voluntary work with the homeless of Los Angeles. She said it was the worst experience she had ever had, and would prefer prison. In fact her request was granted and she served the remainder of her short sentence in gaol. A *calculative contract* is where we are involved because we are paid, in which case money ensures a minimum of performance and obedience. And a *co-operative contract* is where we are involved because we sympathise with the goals of the agency and where we expect to be asked, not ordered, to do things.[18] As Handy points out:

> Voluntary organisations should, by definition, operate under co-operative psychological contracts, but it isn't always easy to remember that this contract gives people the right not to do something. Under pressure it is tempting for those in charge to revert to coercive or at least a calculative contract in order to get things done the way they want them as quickly as possible. Perhaps one reason why those in charge of voluntary organisations can come to prefer working with paid staff than volunteers is that a calculative contract is much easier to operate.[19]

Handy is pointing to the growth in the bureaucratic way of doing things.

The growth of bureaucracies, with paid workers and professional outlooks, is a seemingly unstoppable trend. Social welfare work has expanded enormously in the last 20 years to emerge as one of the major employment sectors in the economy. The Thatcher years have had both voluntary agencies and local authorities imitating commercial enterprise. The recent community care proposals look to a 'mixed economy' of welfare where voluntary agencies will have to become more service-oriented to obtain financial support.[20] Volunteer organisers will find that they will have to master another management skill – costing out volunteer labour. One of the few studies we have, shows that for every £1 spent on organising volunteers, £22 is generated in paid-work equivalent. However, costing is difficult – aspects such as management time are often not considered.[21]

Managing Ambiguity

In matching organisational objectives and volunteer objectives, there may be considerable tension. Work by David Billis has drawn attention to how voluntary enterprise often finds itself in an 'ambiguous zone' caught between the formal world of bureaucracy and the informal personal world.[22] He writes:

> In the personal world [social] problems are resolved by relatives, friends, neighbours, on a private basis. It is not usually found necessary or appropriate to establish contractual arrangements between the parties for the resolution of social problems. This does not preclude the State from the need to pass laws governing aspects of the relationships between, for example, parents and children, and it will attempt to enforce laws through its bureaucratic organs. But the overwhelming character of those relationships is that they are inexplicit.[23]

Whereas in the bureaucratic world:

> The fundamental ground rules assume clear-cut differentiation between a large number of statuses such as: employer and employee; employee and non-employee; provider and recipient; chairman [sic] and director; director and manager; manager and subordinates; owners and governing bodies.[24]

Drawing the worlds as overlapping ovals, we can see the ambiguous zone emerge (see figure 5.1).

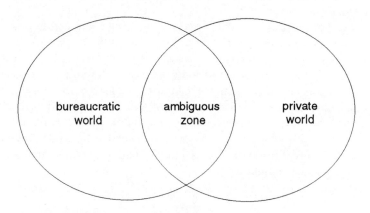

Figure 5.1

The concept of ambiguity serves as a powerful analytical tool. Although Billis uses the model to explain tension in voluntary agencies, we can see its application to volunteers. Questions which organisers must ask are: is the organisation moving into bureaucratic territory and are the volunteers still in the personal world? As our organiser in the charity above commented, she felt that she had to 'relate' more to the volunteers than to her work colleagues.

In *Action for Care*, a study of 1,000 good neighbour schemes, almost all of which were dependent upon volunteers, Philip Abrams and his co-authors found that the organisers of neighbourhood care groups wanted their schemes to disappear into the informal fabric of the community. Yet to achieve these aims and to set up caring networks meant all the bureaucratic paraphernalia of desks, telephone rotas, insurance cover, the taking of references and liaison with welfare professionals.[25] As someone who worked with the co-ordinators of such schemes for five years, I was conscious of the worries and strains they, and their volunteers, experienced from being caught in both worlds.

A recent publication highlights how this tension can arise in the way volunteer organisers have to approach equal opportunities policy. To be successful, EOP policies have to be rigorous and formal (documentation and procedures) – this clashes with volunteer expectations. Yet for the organiser to use more informal ways to be proactive in terms of EOP, setting up sub-groups, for example, may be frowned upon by the agency's management.[26] Recognising that this ambiguity has to be managed, and that it will not go away is the key to being not only a better-equipped volunteer organiser, but a less-stressed one.

For a humorous look at an organisation using volunteers in which ambiguity was rife, I refer the reader to Norman Longmate's, *The Real Dad's Army*.[27] The Home Guard was a volunteer army of over 1,000,000 men at its peak. At the beginning, rules and regulations were imprecise – as was authority. Ambiguity and comedy reigned, as the scriptwriters of *Dad's Army* showed. Interestingly, as the Home Guard became more professional and more like a real army, volunteers drifted away. But this also happened at the same time as the main threat of German invasion receded, so perhaps there was less of a cause to fight for?

Volunteer Organiser Approaches

In terms of the volunteer organiser job, there is likely to be a combination of two broad approaches: the *supervisor approach*, and the *personnel manager approach*. Sometimes these may appear to be at odds with each other. At its basic level, we would have: 'the job must get done, and done well' (supervisor approach); or 'volunteer needs are paramount, we need to find the right job' (personnel manager approach).

As I have argued, successful matching should mean that these two approaches do not conflict. A concentration on the 'job' may lead to exploitation; a concentration on volunteers' needs may mean that many volunteers remain unused. The balance of approach is often revealed in the way volunteers are recruited and inducted. Some organisers aim for high recruitment rates risking wastage at the placement stage: 'If they like it they'll stay, if they don't, well, we'll find someone else.'

The other approach may mean that no volunteer can be deployed, unless the right placement has been set up, and the right support systems are in place. The support system can be labour-intensive. Here is an example from a guide on finding and keeping volunteers:

> A volunteer was placed with a group who had just started to meet in the community hall on an estate. The idea of the placement was as a bridge between a student who worked with the group developing its own identity and being able to organise itself. It appeared after a few meetings that the group only wanted to meet to play bingo. The volunteer's organisational and development capabilities were not used or needed. He felt superfluous to it all. Initially, support was offered by putting the volunteer in touch with the student placement, and they and the Volunteer Organiser discussed the volunteer's role. All were clear about the bridging nature of the placement which was to be time limited, with review built in. The volunteer was introduced to the group; regular checks on progress were made, and signs appeared early of the volunteer not being needed. The volunteer was approached about pulling out, with a sense of dignity and with no feeling of having failed. The situation was explained to the club members, supporting the volunteer's relationship with the group. The volunteer left the group, who were able to cope with organising bingo for themselves.[28]

As well as drawing our attention to the time commitment involved in organising and managing volunteers – often forgotten when cost savings are bandied about – it shows how volunteers in certain contexts can be treated like social work clients. In this case, one wonders why the task ever came to the volunteer in the first place; or

whether the group was really consulted, or its wishes really under-
stood by the volunteer organiser. One also wonders why the
volunteer's 'organisational and development capabilities' were not
successfully applied in the service of bingo.

In allowing for volunteer needs, volunteer organisers may have to
alter the nature of the service on offer. This is particularly relevant in
statutory health and social services settings where volunteering,
whatever its form, is seen as an occupational therapy. Consider this
quote from a volunteer organiser for a social services area office:

> I have 70 volunteers on my books. About 20 of them have
> placements – visiting elderly people. As for the rest, I can't place
> them. I have to keep them occupied with regular meetings and
> social events. To be frank they have been mostly dumped on me.
> They mostly have a history of mental illness, and social workers
> feel voluntary work will help. But what sort of voluntary work? I
> have tried to place them. I have tried to say 'no'. It's difficult. In
> fact I'm running a day club for people with special needs – but I
> haven't got the resources and skills to do that. I'm certainly not
> organising voluntary work.

This quote vividly shows up the pressure on organisers to meet
organisation needs (social workers who refer people on) without any
reference to the true needs of the individual volunteer nor of the real
opportunities available. However, this type of pressure is quite
typical.

The Range of Skills a Volunteer Organiser Will Need

So far we have considered the volunteer and the placement. In this
last section, we shall look at the role of volunteer organisers.

One of the few studies that exists on volunteer organisers was
undertaken in 1987 by the London-based Voluntary Service Co-
ordinators group.[29] The study was based on a survey of 43 organisers
and their voluntary service departments. The report highlights how
varied the job of an organiser can be.

This is how the research report summed up the organiser's job:

> She – for the volunteer organiser is likely to be a woman – works
> in a small department with between one to two workers, in a
> hospital which has around 560 beds. She will have around 140

volunteers on her books, all of whom will generate approximately 326 hours of voluntary service in a week, equivalent to
9 full-time staff members in post. In addition the volunteer
organiser will liaise with three other voluntary groups in the
hospital, spending about 10 per cent of her time on such work.
She will also have responsibility for liaising with at least 2
agencies such as schools, and be responsible for 10 agency
placements covering 41 hours a week, equivalent to just over 1
full-time member of staff. She may be lucky enough to have
administrative support; but the chances are she won't. Adding
up all her volunteer and staff responsibility gives her a team of 12
workers doing a 37-hour week each.

The research produced an interesting table (see table 5.2) on how
organisers recruited, deployed and supervised their volunteers.

Twenty-six (60 per cent) of the departments had a policy on
volunteers; and 39 (91 per cent) took references, the majority of
whom asked for two written references. Sixteen departments (37 per
cent) took extra safeguards regarding children or other 'at risk'
groups – this was before police checks were mandatory. Only eight
(19 per cent) required volunteers to complete a health form. Forty (93
per cent) of the departments gave travel and meal expenses. Twenty-
five (58 per cent) gave induction training, with a similar number
ensuring follow-up training. Thirteen (30 per cent) usually had their
volunteers wearing uniforms. It was found that while 26 departments
had a policy on volunteers, only nine of them issued it to their new
recruits! Only three departments had agreements with hospital
unions; although half the sample reported good relations with union
officials.

With regard to support and supervision for volunteers, around a
half of the departments (organisers) ensured that there were regular
times when they met their volunteers (either weekly, monthly, or
quarterly); whereas the other half used informal arrangements: 'when
they pop in', or 'over lunch'.

It was found that, in terms of tasks expected from the hospital,
around 35 new requests per month came into the average department.
Nineteen (44 per cent) departments asked for requests to be put into
writing, and seven of those used a request form. Seventeen (40 per
cent) organisers asked for requests to be channelled through a
professional before it could be dealt with. Only three departments
had regular arrangements for reviewing requests, with the person/

Table 5.2 *Aspects of how voluntary service co-ordinators recruit, deploy and supervise volunteers*

Size of Voluntary Service Co-ordinator Department — Number of organisers working in the department

	Up to 0.99	1.0 – 1.99	2.0 – 2.99	3.0 and over	Total
Number surveyed	4	24	5	10	43
Percentage	9%	56%	12%	23%	100%
Average size	0.5	1.0	2.0	3.3	1.6
Recruiting Volunteers					
Policy on volunteers	1	14	4	7	26
Percentage	25%	58%	80%	70%	60%
One reference	1	5	0	2	8
Two references	2	18	5	6	31
No references	1	1	0	2	4
Extra safeguards	2	9	1	4	16
Health form	0	4	0	4	8
Deploying Volunteers					
Copy of policy	1	7	1	0	9
Travel expenses	4	23	5	8	40
Meal allowances	4	23	5	8	40
Induction training	2	13	4	6	25
Other training	3	11	3	7	24
Uniforms	0	9	0	4	13
Supervision					
Regular times	1	12	4	3	20
Informal	3	11	1	7	22

Source: London Hospital Based Voluntary Services Co-ordinators Group, *A Survey of Voluntary Service Departments in Hospitals* (ADVANCE, 1987).

unit sponsoring the request. Thirty-three (92 per cent of the 36 who answered this question) relied on informal arrangements. Only 10 (23 per cent) of the organisers themselves received regular supervision. They were effectively working on their own.

The report commented on the lack of recognition by health authorities of the importance of the organisers' role in terms of work output and benefit to hospitals. Given the great responsibility they carry, the report commented on the low salary, and lack of career status and opportunity that organisers have when compared with other managerial jobs in health and social services.

The lack of recognition experienced by hospital volunteer organisers applies to most other volunteer co-ordinators. The point must be made, and made strongly, that managing volunteers is, in many cases, more difficult, and requires more skill, than managing paid staff.

A Check List for Managing and Organising Volunteers

This brief survey has looked at a number of issues relevant to organising volunteers. In this final section, a check list is given on using volunteers in organisations. In the first part of the list questions are identified; in the second part, information and advice is given.

Some Questions Your Agency May Ask

1 Why does the agency want to use volunteers/is using volunteers?
- Is the agency philosophically committed to using volunteers for some particular reason? For example, the citizens advice bureaux movement is committed to using volunteers to ensure community representation and to insure equality between client and advisor.
- Is the use of volunteers the only viable way of organising the service on offer – say, with a local good neighbour scheme?
- Or are volunteers seen as a stop-gap until money can be secured to buy in paid workers?
- Is the agency's growth dependent on volunteers?

2 Are clearly definable jobs identified in the work of the organisation?
- Are there jobs within the organisation that can be spelt out in a brief job description/person specification?
- What is the balance between jobs which are 'doable' for volunteers, and 'doable' for paid staff?

3 Is the agency committed fully to equal opportunities?
- Is there fairness in getting volunteers involved, irrespective of their gender, race, age, sexual orientation, religion, marital status, disability, or tribal origin?
- Has the agency taken practical steps to ensure that practice on fairness is properly monitored to ensure that no discrimination takes place in terms of advertising, recruitment, deployment and support?

4 Is there a system for interviewing and selection?
- When interviewing and selecting volunteers, have prospective recruits been given full information on what the agency has to offer and the criteria for selection?

5 Are references expected?
- Do volunteers need to supply references? For work with children in certain contexts, police checks may be necessary.

6 Are job descriptions and terms and conditions of service issued?
- When deployed, are volunteers given a job description and a briefing note giving information on their entitlement and on the agency?

7 What is the review period for the placement?
- Is an induction period relevant to the volunteer?
- Is there a review period for the placement?

8 How will the placement be supervised?
- Does the volunteer know to whom he or she is accountable, or to whom he or she should look to for advice and support?
- Does the volunteer know the grievance and disciplinary process in the agency – to senior management or management committee?

9 Is relevant training on offer?
- Is training on offer to extend the volunteer's skills?
- Does the organiser ensure that job variety and job change are regularly assessed?

10 Are necessary expenses offered?
- Is the volunteer aware of the expenses on offer, and how to claim?

11 Is help given to volunteers on benefits?
- Is the volunteer who is receiving state benefits advised fully on the implications of his or her involvement?

12 Have legal and insurance aspects been taken care of?
- Are all legal aspects with regard to volunteers adequately covered?

13 How is the volunteer's performance assessed?
- Is there a formal system?

- What measures are used?

14 Does the volunteer have the right of representation and access to union or professional association help?
- Is the agency's policy with regard to a volunteer's membership of a union or professional association clear?
- Does the agency support union or association membership by providing a fund to pay appropriate fees?
- Does the volunteer have the right to attend paid staff, or committee meetings?

15 Does the management committee know what rules determine volunteer involvement?
- Are management committee members given copies of the relevant Memorandum of Articles for the Charity (or relevant constitutional papers)?
- Are they given support, as outlined above?

16 Does the volunteer organiser know whether he or she is principally a supervisor or a personnel officer?
- What is the role of the organiser in the organisation? Does he or she determine the rate of work (tasks requested/volunteers recruited) or not?
- At what management level is he or she in the management of the organisation?

Some Information

1 Paid staff and volunteers
Guidelines for Relationships between Volunteers and Paid Non-Professional Workers (the Drain Guidelines)[30] outlines when and where volunteers should be used vis-à-vis paid workers, and gives guidance on the role of volunteers in industrial disputes. The guidelines have the backing of several major unions.

2 Equal Opportunities
Legislation for paid workers is laid down in:
- the Race Relations Act 1976
- the Sex Discrimination Acts 1975 and 1986
- the Equal Pay Act 1970
- the Disabled (Employment) Acts 1944 and 1958.

This legislation does not apply to volunteers, but should be used as a starting point for adopting a policy position. The ADVANCE report, *Equal Opportunities and Volunteering* comments that: 'Other legislation such as that relating to the prohibition of promoting gay and lesbian lifestyles (section 28 of the 1988 Local Government Act) has an effect on the climate in which volunteering takes place, though it does not refer to volunteers.'[31]

3 Risks and Hazards
Volunteers deployed may:

- be injured by accidents or physical assault
- may lose or damage their property
- may injure, by accident or physical assault, members of the public (clients) or their property
- damage or lose the property of members of the public (clients)

Under the Occupiers Liability Act 1957, any agency with premises must make sure that visitors are safe. Under the Health and Safety at Work Act 1974, an organisation which employs staff is obliged to secure the health and safety of non-employees who may be affected by their activities.

4 Reasonable care and references
Organisations must always demonstrate that they have taken 'reasonable care' over the selection, supervision and training of volunteers and their use of equipment. References may have to be taken – should they be written, or verbal? Should the potential volunteer be visited at home?

5 Work with children
Statutory authorities are required to make a police check on those working with children. As yet, this does not apply to voluntary agencies, although a pilot scheme is in operation. However, considerable care must be taken with references. For further advice contact The Volunteer Centre UK.

6 Insurance
Insurance can be secured to cover most contingencies:

- Public Liability will cover the organisation against claims by people other than employees arising from accidents that cause injury, or damage.

- Employers' Liability covers employees from claims from third parties.
- Contingent Liability, in addition to volunteer drivers' own motor insurance, will ensure organisational cover for excess on claims, and volunteers may have their 'no claims bonus' covered.
- Professional Indemnity Insurance covers an organisation which has volunteers (staff) giving advice, which may result in a claim.

7 Expenses
- Who within the agency is to receive expenses – all volunteers, or just management committee members?
- What expenses should be covered – travel, telephone, car mileage, entertainment?
- At what rate – what the agency can afford, or tied to a national rate such as used by local authorities?
- How do expenses fit in with DSS rules? Get a copy of the DSS leaflet, *Voluntary Work and Social Security*.
- How are expenses administered – does everyone receive expenses, those not wanting to claim having the opportunity to decline?
- Should expenses be in kind?
- Lots of socials and outings may be more valuable than small amounts of cash paid to individuals.

8 Union or Professional Association Membership
- Will the organisation assist in the payment of dues? Volunteers on benefit can offset union subscriptions as a reasonable expense. The union, Manufacturing, Science and Finance (MSF) offers a free union membership scheme for volunteers.

For further information refer to the leaflets: *All Expenses Paid*, and *Protecting Volunteers*, available from The Volunteer Centre UK, 29 Lower King's Road, Berkhamsted, Herts HP4 2AB, tel. 0442-873311; and, *Voluntary But Not Amateur, A Guide to the Law for Voluntary Organisations and Community Groups*, available from the London Voluntary Service Council, 68 Chalton Street, London NW1 1JR, tel. 071-388 0241. For advice on equal opportunities and black involvement, contact the Resource Unit to Promote Black Volunteering, Unit 117–119, Brixton Enterprise Centre, 444 Brixton Road, London SW9 8ES, tel. 071-738 3462.

CHAPTER 6

COMMUNITY ORGANISATIONS AND VOLUNTARY ACTION

Colin Rochester

Introduction

This chapter sets out to chart some of the relatively unfamiliar territory that is to be found between organised volunteering, on the one side, and self-help on the other. For want of a more satisfactory term, I shall call this the world of community organisations. The text below places this 'world' in a context; describes its main characteristics; looks at some examples of this kind of voluntary action; and draws conclusions about its significance.

Voluntary action takes place in a variety of organisational contexts. At one end of the range is the formal world of bureaucracy with its 'rule book' to govern all activities and its clear-cut distinctions of status and function. At the other end is the equally familiar informal or private world which we share with our family and friends. And in between these poles is what David Billis has described as the 'ambiguous zone'.[1] Here bureaucracy and the private world are seen to overlap and here we find the natural habitat of many voluntary organisations. They do not belong in the private world where ideas, such as membership, different statuses and functions, and management and accountability have no place. At the same time, they are not bureaucracies because they lack the clear-cut distinctions that are central to bureaucratic organisations, such as those between employer and employee, employee and non-employee, provider and recipient, and manager and subordinate.

If the range of contexts for voluntary action is seen as a spectrum running from the bureaucratic to the private via various kinds of 'ambiguous' arrangements, we can place the world of organised volunteering squarely at or near the formal end of the sequence. Some takes place within statutory agencies, such as social services departments or hospitals which are organised as bureaucracies. The larger voluntary agencies which deploy volunteers are organised on similar lines. And, increasingly, other voluntary agencies have taken a bureaucratic approach to voluntary work. A model of good practice has been developed which treats the volunteer as an unpaid employee. That is to say, that the volunteer's role is specified in a job description and his or her rights and responsibilities are defined in some kind of contract. Arrangements are made for induction, supervision, support and training. There are two considerations underlying this approach. Firstly, the volunteer represents a resource to the organisation which it must use efficiently in furthering activities which have been determined before the volunteer is recruited. Secondly, the voluntary contribution must be 'rewarded' by the satisfaction of the volunteer's needs for personal growth and the acquisition of new skills and knowledge.

By contrast, self-help is found at the private and informal end of the spectrum. Self-help groups are formed of people who share a particular condition or problem. Within these groups, there is no meaningful distinction between givers and receivers: relationships are reciprocal. The activities of the group are chosen after it has come together and by a process of decision-making by consensus. There are few 'rules' and little, if any, differentiation of roles and statuses.

In between these two models of voluntary action lies the fundamentally ambiguous world of community organisations. What are their main characteristics? In the first place, they are organisations which are formally constituted with specified aims, a collection of rules by which their affairs are to be administered, and distinct roles for their officers and committees. Typically they are associations, directed through democratic procedures by their own membership. Unlike private clubs, however, community organisations extend the offer of membership to whole populations – typically of a neighbourhood or a housing estate – without distinction of age, race, gender, or religion. They may or may not employ staff.

Within this framework of organisation, there remain some important areas of ambiguity that distinguish the community organisation from the bureaucratic model. Firstly, the distinction between those who provide services or run activities and those who consume them is not clear. Members may be active or passive, or both. Secondly, there is no differentiation between those who make decisions and those who carry them out. Officers and committee members tend to be expected to undertake the work of the organisation as well as to guide its affairs. But they may well be joined in the work by other members who are not part of the committee.

Thirdly, there is no clear-cut distinction between paid staff (where they exist) and voluntary workers.

Voluntary action in the world of community organisations is, therefore, a different experience from organised volunteering. People are not typically recruited to play specific roles in the pursuit of activities that have already been designed. Instead, they become involved in some way with an organisation that offers a range of opportunities to play a part in planning its work and carrying it forward. The volunteer's eventual role in the organisation may well be a product not only of personal interests and skills but also of negotiation and pure accident. And the motivation and rewards for involvement are less to do with personal development and more to do with a sense of shared purpose. Working with others towards a valued goal is rewarded by fellowship and brings a feeling of 'ownership' of the organisation and its work.

Community Associations

One significant manifestation of this form of voluntary action in Britain is the community association movement.[2] This was a product of the massive housebuilding programme to provide 'homes fit for heroes' after the First World War. In the 1920s, tens of thousands of people were uprooted and relocated some miles away in vast new municipal housing estates on the edge of the cities. The result was the formation of extensive single-class enclaves of low-income families (all the more so, since they needed to find the cost of travel to work) with few, if any, amenities. The response to these conditions on the LCC's Dagenham and Watling estates, and on similar developments in the provinces, was the establishment of community centres 'based on a wide and varied membership which shall foster and serve as a focus for the social life of the whole community'.[3]

The idea of forming community associations to develop and manage community centres spread rapidly. By 1937 the National Council of Social Service was in contact with 170 towns in which community centres were either in existence or planned. A year later the figure had reached 304. After the Second World War numbers continued to grow, slowly at first but accelerating during the 1960s. The 929 centres of 1960 had become 1,700 three years later and, by 1980, it was estimated that there were something of the order of 2,500 community associations in Britain with a total membership of around half a million people.

These figures do not include the large numbers of tenants' associations and other estate-based groups that developed during the 1960s and 1970s. While they shared some of the purposes of the community associations, they generally failed to meet the acid test of a constitutional commitment to addressing all the needs of a neighbourhood which was seen as the distinguishing feature of the community association.

Essentially, community associations aim to serve identifiable neighbourhoods of some thousands of households. A comparatively small proportion of the local population will become members and an even smaller percentage will play an active role in their affairs. The earliest associations were formed to provide some focus for uprooted communities and to enable people to make contact with other residents. More recent developments have sprung from concern about some specific local issue or from the expressed need for somewhere to house leisure-time activities, especially for children and young people.

Once established, community associations meet a number of needs. Members join in order to pursue a hobby, or to promote a cause, or for the opportunity to make contact with other people. The associations, however, have a track record which goes beyond the purely social and recreational. They have seen their work both as an informal means of providing education to people who would not set foot in a more formal setting, and as a practical training ground for democracy. They can perhaps be seen as a breeding ground for 'active citizens', 1920s style!

All this stems from the view that the purpose of the community association is to promote the welfare of the whole community. An unpublished paper from the early 1970s sets out what this means:[4]

a. to bring individuals together (to foster the spirit of community)

b. to bring together . . . organisations in the locality

c. to provide opportunities for leisure time activities in response to local needs (to provide opportunities for the creative use of leisure)

d. to provide a basis for an education in democratic practice (training for democracy and citizenship)

e. to see that gaps in community service are filled

f. to manage the community centre

g. to provide a corporate voice for the local community.

It is not suprising that reality tends to fall well short of this lofty ambition. One of the pioneers of the movement, Sir Wyndham Deedes, commended the idea 'even if . . . there is nowhere an example of a completely successful community association or centre'.[5] Forty years later, the general secretary of the National Federation of Community Associations suggested that no more than 5 per cent of their members made a serious attempt to address that kind of programme: 'Management of the centre and the development of leisure time activities are enough to fill their time.'[6] But the idea remains alive: the 1989 conference of the National Federation was entirely devoted to strategies for 'reaching out' in pursuit of the associations' wider roles.

The attempt to meet these goals has been made, on the whole, by voluntary workers. While most community centres will have a paid warden (and some of them may also have an assistant), the movement has never attracted outside funding from statutory or private sources on a large scale. As a result, not only is the association owned and governed by its members but it is also heavily dependent on their voluntary efforts to carry out its operational tasks. The one or more paid staff involved facilitiate the work of the organisation, and share the duties with the active members rather than carry them out on behalf of the membership.

If the achievements of community associations fall short of the ideal, they remain considerable. One way of measuring them is to list

the tasks completed and the groups which have been helped. Arts and drama projects produce their exhibitions and their plays. Green belts have been preserved, motorways diverted and housing improved . . . People of different ethnic origins have found a place to meet and talk to each other. The take-up rates for social security have been improved.[7]

Another method is to look at the extent to which the movement has engaged the active involvement of its members.

While there has been an inevitable variation from association to association and an 'ebb and flow' over time, the community association movement has produced a significant group of leaders at local, regional and national level who have shown great vigour and stamina. They 'have so often proved to be enterprising neighbours and tireless workers for their communities'.[8] While they will have become involved and have stayed involved – at least in part – because they have gained personal satisfaction and individual growth from their participation, they were – and are – also moved by other motives. For them, the improvement of the welfare of the community is a worthy objective to be pursued with like-minded colleagues in a venture which they feel belongs to them.

A Community-Based Youth Project

The growth of community organisations and community development work in the 1960s and 1970s provided the conditions for a pioneering approach to the provision of facilities and activities for children and young people in south London's inner city.[9] Cambridge House – the Cambridge University Settlement in Camberwell – was an early proponent of community work, employing a full-time worker in 1967 to stimulate the formation of tenants' associations and other groups, and to provide them with continuing support.

This appointment coincided with something of a crisis in the affairs of the Settlement's Boys Club. The Georgian house which had provided its premises for the past 30 years was not only in need of repair and renovation, but was also regarded as unsuitable and badly placed. It was difficult to find a skilled and experienced leader. The users voted with their feet and attendances dwindled to the point at which the club was closed.

After some deliberation, Cambridge House decided to follow the then fashionable trend in youth work away from 'building centred' and towards 'detached' work. But the experience of the community development worker pointed them in a direction that was rather different to the usual detached work model. Instead of employing a youth worker to work face-to-face with young people on the streets, or wherever they were to be found, it was decided to appoint someone with a community development brief. Through the existing community groups, he or she would make contact with adults living on the local estates, and encourage them to design and run activities and projects for the young people in their communities.

The choice of this method was prompted by the scale and the nature of the problem. 'Detached work' of the normal pattern would only reach the small number of children whom the worker could work with face-to-face. The population of children and young people on the local estates was large, and the facilities for recreation and play woefully inadequate. As a result, there was considerable friction and conflict between the children and the adults on the estates. Furthermore, some tenants' groups had run small-scale activities for children: a summer play scheme here, a football team there. Thus the worker would stimulate, support and advise groups to organise these kind of activities, and others on a larger scale.

The first worker was appointed in 1972 and, five years later, was joined by a second. By Autumn 1983, it was estimated that some 400 children and young people were taking part in the project's activities. This was made possible by the involvement of more than 50 local adults. While some of the five estates served by the work achieved more and involved more adults than others, all had achievements to report. Commitment was sustained for quite long periods – it is easy to underestimate the amount of work involved by volunteers in keeping a club running for two years or organising an inter-estate five-a-side football league for five years. And while the quality of the volunteers' work varied – some learned lessons the hard way, others showed considerable organisational skills – a similar inconsistency can be found in the work of paid staff in the youth service.

The quantity of provision achieved by the project was clearly greater than that which could have been provided by two professionals working directly and without mobilising local support. Moreover, the quality was arguably comparable with other provision. At the same time, the project claimed that the approach brought other dividends. In the first place, it meant a growth of understanding between the generations – adults began to see young people differently as they came to know them, and young people began to take a different view of the adults. The result was a greater sense of community on the estates which was demonstrated by a decrease in the level of vandalism. Secondly, the project offered local adults a chance to acquire skills in human relations and in organisation. Finally, local people were frequently better informed about the activities that would interest the children. One estate now has a majorette troupe which has been hugely successful. How many professional youth workers would have put that at the top of their lists of possible activities?

Despite these achievements, the method did have some difficulties and limitations. Voluntary action cannot be sustained indefinitely. Community groups are fragile. Support for them will rise and fall and, from time to time, they will be riven by dissension. Some young people needed more intensive and skilled support than could be provided through this approach. For the paid workers, the biggest problem was to restrain themselves from interfering. The essence of the method was that local people should not only carry out the tasks, but also make the decisions about what to do and how to organise it.

As a result, there were 'times when the workers could see that a group were heading for chaos but their advice was not heeded. They then had to sit back and watch it happen'.[10] Nor was job satisfaction easily gained: if an activity was a success the credit tended to go to the volunteers who had organised it.

Nonetheless, in the harsh world of the high-density estates of the inner city, a considerable volume of effective voluntary action was mobilised to improve the quality of life for children and adults alike. The recipe for its success combined ownership of the work by local people (which meant that they designed and delivered the service) with skilled and unobtrusive support and advice from the professional workers.

Adventure Playgrounds

Another form of provision for children in the disadvantaged areas of our cities is adventure playgrounds. Originally known as 'junk' playgrounds when the idea first reached Britain just after the Second World War, their revised title can also be misleading. The 'adventure' in the play that takes place on the playgrounds is less to do with the large structures and ropeways many of them feature than with their view that their activities should be determined by the young users themselves. The playground is seen as a flexible resource which can adapt to changing needs and offer a wide range of activities, including indoor painting and craftwork as well as outdoor play.

Playgrounds serve very local or neighbourhood catchment areas and see themselves as accountable to their local community. Historically, they are the creation of community activists who have established the need for provision, and have persuaded local authorities to provide them with the means of employing paid staff. Today the affairs of the adventure playground associations which they founded are directed by a committee elected at an annual general meeting by their local constituency, and their work is largely delegated to paid playworkers. Thus they appear to have taken on many of the characteristics of the almost bureaucratic voluntary agency with its distinctions between employer and employee, and between those who make decisions and those who carry them out. In practice, however, the position is less clear.

In the past, much of the work of the playgrounds' London federation – the London Adventure Playgrounds Association or LAPA – has been aimed at supporting and training the paid workers on local playgrounds whose status, pay and conditions of service have been poor. Recently, the organisation has become aware that gains in professionalism have been accompanied by a loss of community involvement and voluntary activity, on the one hand, and increased pressures on voluntary management committees on the other. At the suggestion of staff of the Calouste Gulbenkian Foundation and with the help of a grant from the National Children's Play and Recreation Unit, LAPA entered into a partnership with Community Service Volunteers (CSV) to run a small-scale demonstration project which would address this problem.

The People for Play project aimed to draw on CSV's expertise to develop models for the increased and improved involvement of volunteers in adventure playgrounds. Due to a number of unforeseen circumstances, the modest resources 'budgeted' for the project were not, in the event, all made available and the lessons drawn from it need to be treated with caution. Nonetheless, its findings contain important lessons not only for adventure playgrounds but also for a wider range of organisations.

The project was focused on the adaptation for playground use of the models used in the world of organised volunteering. These can be separated into two areas: recruitment and deployment. The project developed a complete recruitment package to help the two participating playgrounds deal with the response to advertisements placed in a well-known listings magazine. This included a two-page application form, provision for taking up two references, informal visits and a formal interview. In the same vein, the project created tools for the deployment and supervision of volunteers which included job descriptions and contracts, guidelines for induction, supervision and training, and arrangements for assessment and review of the progress of the individual volunteer. This experience forms the basis of an information pack for dissemination to LAPA's member playgrounds.

The People for Play project, however, also identified an alternative approach to recruiting and retaining voluntary workers which seems more in harmony with the origins of the playgrounds as community organisations. Rather than treating the volunteer as an unpaid employee with personal needs, this approach deals with potential voluntary workers as members of the community who 'own' the playground. While their voluntary work may well reward them with personal development, the greater incentives are derived from joining with other people from their own community to maintain and develop a valued facility.

The method is informal and can be described as 'organic'. One of the playground workers involved with the project described this as encouraging people to 'drop in for a chat' and generally 'lend a hand'. Initial interest of this kind could then be developed into an increasing contribution to the work and management of the playground. This process of recruitment rapidly shades into a method of deploying the volunteers. There is no preconceived 'job' which they are requested to take on. Instead, the individual volunteer will explore the range of possible roles and choose one or more that he or she feels comfortable with. And, since what is on offer is a share in the ownership of the playground, the volunteers have opportunities to shape the future work of the project by sharing decision-making as well as helping to organise its activities and to maintain the organisation.

The People for Play project was a modest exploratory study but it suggests strongly that, while the more conventional model of organised volunteering might have its place on adventure playgrounds, the informal approach summarised here appears to be more relevant to the needs of small, community-based organisations.

A Different Kind of Community

Another glimpse of the alternative model of volunteering in relatively informal voluntary organisations is provided by a recent study in which Peter Tihanyi looked at the characteristics and the motives and rewards for volunteers in three Jewish day centres for elderly people.[11]

He found that the great majority of the 200 or so volunteers were themselves elderly (most of them aged over 70) and Jewish. They were also similar in status, income and education to the users of the centres. While the principal incentive was personal – to fill a gap in their own lives and, most notably, the one left by the death of a partner – they were also motivated by feelings of solidarity with the users. It was important to them that the centres served the Jewish community.

The great majority of the volunteers were recruited by personal contact. They were introduced by friends, or were part of a network involved in the day centre. And they chose the centre as a place to do voluntary work because it was geographically convenient, or because it was situated in an area where they had grown up and where they felt their roots were.

Having recruited large numbers of volunteer staff in this way, the centres were very successful in keeping them. Typically, volunteers' careers were measured in years. Tihanyi suggests that they stayed because they took pride in the contribution which they were making to the work. They enjoyed the social benefits of mixing with people and they were rewarded by the appreciation expressed informally by both users and colleagues. The 'essential ingredient' in achieving such a high level of volunteer satisfaction was the definition of the individual's role. This was done by assigning the volunteer to a particular department with specific functions. It was important that it was the department rather than the individual that carried the 'job description'. (Some volunteers had been issued with detailed job descriptions but had torn them up.) This way of defining the role gave direction to the work and limited personal responsibility without subjecting volunteers to the kind of detailed supervision which they felt was irksome. And, for some, it offered room to develop their own interpretation of the role.

The absence of job descriptions was paralleled by the lack of formal systems of support, supervision and training. Volunteers felt that they received a great deal of support, but this operated in a very informal manner. There was a clear distinction between managers (paid staff in two of the centres, members of the committee in the other) and the volunteers, but management was not allowed to become intrusive: instructions were delivered in the form of requests and consultation. Training was conspicuous by its absence and the volunteers' opinions were divided about whether it was necessary or desirable.

These three day centres appear to have attracted and retained large numbers of volunteer staff without using the model of volunteering that treats voluntary workers as unpaid employees. While providing a more structured environment than the other examples I have discussed, they also left considerable space for the volunteers to create their own roles and to make their own judgement about when and where to seek support. Crucially, they attracted people through personal networks and drew from a community with shared values. While volunteers had personal needs to meet, much of their motivation and job satisfaction was derived from playing their part in a community venture.

Conclusion

These examples of voluntary action in community-based organi-sations provide, I hope, rather more than four interesting snap-shots of life in the ambiguous zone of comparatively informal voluntary bodies. They also provide a glimpse of a model of voluntary action which is in some danger of being obscured by the 'organised volunteering' approach of the bureaucratic world.

Its main features are set out below:

- It draws volunteers from the community served by the organisation.
- It gives them a share in the 'ownership' of the project, or activity, or service.
- It can involve volunteers not only in performing the operational tasks of the organisation but also in defining its purpose and setting its goals.
- It suggests a range of roles for paid staff who may be advisers or partners rather than managers.
- It gives volunteers the opportunities to create their own roles.
- It tries to provide an education in 'practical democracy' as well as a training in skills.

Its problems as an approach are:

- Its outcomes can be unpredictable and erratic.
- It involves taking risks. This presents a difficulty for paid staff who operate in this way.
- Staff are reluctant to concede power to volunteers.

On the other hand, it has some proven success as a method of mobilising substantial, energetic and creative voluntary action. It is high time that this model of voluntary action was rescued from neglect and its contribution to society was given the recognition that is due to it.

CHAPTER 7

BLACK PEOPLE AND VOLUNTEERING

David Obaze

Introduction

Hands up those who think that black people *don't* volunteer. Well, the fact is, they do, and that should not be surprising. Black people have a great passion for volunteering. It is an addiction that can lie dormant until it is revived by asking. But it seems to be the case that white people don't ask. But to whom do I refer when I say black? I mean people of the Commonwealth countries, Africa, and those with Afro-Caribbean and Asian backgrounds, and all those who think that they are discriminated against by white people because they are not white.

It is pardonable to think that black people are hidden from active volunteering. Until recently, it was generally accepted that volunteering was a white preserve. The 1981 major survey on volunteering[1] found that 44 per cent of the population was involved in some form of volunteering activity at any one time. The survey found that volunteers were likely to be people who:

- were educated to further or higher education level
- were in a white-collar job
- were owner-occupier householders
- owned and drove a car
- had a telephone
- had children
- were aged between 35 and 44, and
- were white

As in many other activities, black people are hidden or literally not counted in the statistics. A survey carried out by the major research organisation MORI in 1990 discovered that:

> In all 3 per cent of the sample were from ethnic minorities, less than the national figure of 5 per cent of the British population. This is probably because ethnic minorities tend to be concentrated in major cities and the 'omnibus' survey is carried out using a randomly spread nationwide sample.[2]

We do have some research evidence on black volunteering. It should be noted, however, that to get that evidence a pressure group had to be set up. The Black Perspectives in Volunteering Group undertook the first-ever survey into black volunteering in 1988.[3] In total, 162 black people were interviewed in five London boroughs. The sample was structured so that approximately equal numbers of people from the Afro-Caribbean, African and Asian communities were interviewed. Also the sample was structured to cover a range of volunteering involvement: people who were presently involved in what they called voluntary work; people who had previously been in voluntary work; and those who had never been involved in volunteering.

A Profile of Black Volunteering

In establishing a profile of black volunteers – both current and past – the survey found that, for the most part, features affecting their involvement were similar to features affecting white volunteers.

The sample of black volunteers were motivated by wanting to help, to care, to give – satisfying what might be called aspects of their 'inner-self'. They were mostly involved in neighbourhood care activities, such as shopping, babysitting and visiting the elderly; and they found out about volunteering through friends. They were usually working with one organisation; and were committed to their volunteering, with around a half having been involved in their activity for over three years. The majority of the black volunteers were in employment; women had similar volunteering profiles to men; and most black volunteers preferred to be involved in their local neighbourhoods.

All these statements could have been said about a sample of white volunteers. However, there were differences. With regard to motivation, a quarter of the black volunteers wanted to 'meet needs'. The way 'needs' were perceived and met were shown in answers to other questions. There was a strong interest in advice and advocacy work, and several respondents had founded the organisations in which they were involved. Comments about need were: 'to help my people', 'you can't sit at home and do nothing'.

One question asked in the survey was 'Have you any preference about the racial, religious or cultural make-up of any organisation you volunteer for?' Out of the 162 respondents, 67 per cent said they had no preference. Of these, 42 per cent were Asian; 76 per cent Afro-Caribbean and 82 per cent Africans.

Overall, two-thirds of the sample were open in their attitudes to volunteering, having no preference with regard to ethnic group; yet the survey found that only around half of the black volunteers were actually working in what might be called 'mixed groups'. Taking account of the views expressed on needs, it appears that black volunteers are not finding opportunities for channelling their energies into existing outlets for volunteering – these outlets being agencies which are predominantly white in membership and management. Black people have to look to their own organisations.

The findings suggest that black volunteering is largely about black self-help. Given the black experience in Britain and the battery of statistics which show up the discrimination which black people face, this is hardly surprising. Readers should not forget the legacies of the 1950s 'colour bar', which applied not only to jobs and housing, but was also operated by voluntary agencies, trade unions and churches. Black people have had to become self-reliant.

We can note that the black voluntary sector is thriving. Take as an index, *Bridges*, the directory of ethnic minority community groups in Greater London, which shows how rich in variety and how widespread are black organisations.[4] But the point has to be made that this growth and development appears to be running parallel to the white voluntary sector. We should also note that recent changes in government policy are putting the black voluntary sector under much pressure. We shall return to this issue later in the chapter.

The survey reveals differences within the ethnic community itself. As many as 58 per cent of the Asian sub-sample preferred to work with their own ethnic group and this figure rose to 70 per cent for Asians who had never volunteered. Reasons given were related to religion, language and custom: 'I fear for my culture, my identity', said one respondent.

While, overall, two-thirds of the ethnic respondents were open to working with mixed agencies, a third still preferred their own group.

Outside religion and language, the reasons were, as might be expected, to do with security, feelings of comfort and ease: 'I'm happier with people I know.'

The survey findings fit in well with data on political and trade union black participation, and show that a substantial number of black people feel insecure with what we can call the 'atmosphere' on offer from white agencies. This is the situation even though black people have many of the same concerns as whites. What is worrying about the survey findings is that the sample was biased to younger people – aged 20–39 – the majority of whom would have been schooled in Britain. Attitudes are still clearly entrenched.

Experience of racism was quoted in 12 per cent of the replies. No overt racist incidents were reported, the racism – nowadays euphemistically labelled 'institutional' – was more subtle. For example, a past volunteer's view of a tenants' association was that 'people were very kind and helpful and made me feel at home, but odd remarks were dropped. Nothing specific, but I was always aware – I felt I was being judged for my colour, not for myself. I know they didn't mean it but I didn't feel comfortable.' And a current volunteer, talking about her work in a well-established voluntary agency, said: 'They had the policy alright. But they expected me to be the expert on black matters, and when I wasn't they sort of looked down on me. Comments are made . . . I feel sometimes like I'm just the token black.'

Black people in the survey gave up voluntary work mostly because of changes in their personal circumstances: they had got a job, moved away, or found they didn't have the time. As for agency problems, stress was mentioned in three cases but no one gave up because of racism.

The survey data raises the vexed question of how important is skin colour itself in determining how and why people volunteer. Reviewing the evidence, the Black Perspectives in Volunteering Group made the following points. Firstly, it should be expected that people who know each other and share experience will have an affinity for what they would call their own grouping. The Group quoted the public school fraternity which dominates many British institutions, or the local coal miners' lodge, as typical white examples. Secondly, it was noted that volunteering is biased towards middle-class attributes and, as the socio-economic data show that the majority of the black population is not middle class, it would be expected that black people would have the same reservations and face the same obstacles with regard to volunteering as white working-class people. Thirdly, the Group noted that what counted as volunteering for black people may have been different to what counted as volunteering for white people – or at least the organisers of white organisations. The survey showed a bias towards neighbourhood activities of an informal nature. Black respondents commented that their activities did not receive the financial support that white agencies usually obtained.

Overall, the Black Perspectives in Volunteering Group was of the view that skin colour was a factor in itself in determining involvement in volunteering. If you are black, you are treated differently and you are discriminated against.

Black Experiences of Volunteering

Black volunteers were asked about their experience of volunteering: likes, dislikes, gains and, if they had given up, the reasons why. On likes, most replies were centred around personal satisfaction and achievement. On gains, volunteers pointed to broader life experience and the acquisition of skills.

That volunteering – whether in black or mixed agencies – was a positive experience cannot be denied: over half the sample reported no 'dislikes'. Of the dislikes quoted, around half were to do with the individual's personal circumstances, with worries concerning their time commitments and money. The rest were to do with the agency and the work agenda: 'So much to be done but so little resources.'

Black People Who Are Not Volunteers

The profile of non-volunteers in the sample was biased towards the young – half were aged under 29, and nearly a quarter were unemployed. Reasons for not volunteering centred on lack of information about what was on offer, and not knowing about the right opportunities. Other concerns were about personal circumstances: worries about time, arrangements for the care of dependants, and worries over financial matters, particularly in relation to welfare benefits.

The image of volunteers was referred to by around 10 per cent of the non-volunteers. Questioned further about image, the majority of all the sample said that volunteers were 'middle-class or affluent', but only a few respondents pointed to volunteers being white. Overall, non-volunteers had a fairly open and positive view of volunteering,

seeing gains in 'satisfaction' and 'happiness' from potential involvement. Thirty-six per cent of the non-volunteers said that they had a
preference for their own ethnic group with regard to taking up a
voluntary activity.

Encouraging Black Volunteering: the Survey's Recommendations

The survey gives a number of pointers to white agencies to encourage
black volunteering and to break down discrimination.

It showed that black volunteers are very much the same as white
volunteers and, in many cases, needs and interests overlap. However,
because the black community is in a minority and very thinly spread,
it was noted that it was not easy for volunteering agencies to involve
black people or, on the other hand, it was easy to exaggerate their
differences with regard to white people: 'Often we're simply not
asked', said one respondent. 'I've been told that Muslims behave in a
certain way, no one's asked me and I'm a Muslim', said another. So
one pointer is that volunteer-using agencies must check their
assumptions, and find out what really is going on in the community.

After checking assumptions, agencies should adopt an anti-racist
stance by drawing up policies on work so that good practice on equal
opportunities can be implemented and reviewed. All aspects of work
should be considered, such as publicity and the working atmosphere
of the organisation. The report said: 'Imagine that you are a black
person coming to volunteer – how would you feel stepping into the
office of the agency for the first time?' It was noted that institutional
racism was made by people and that it could be changed. Clearly,
volunteering agencies should aim to put as many people as possible at
their ease.

The survey also found that lack of information was a factor
inhibiting black volunteer involvement. People find out about
volunteering through friends. Having attractive and relevant publicity
was seen to encourage black participation, but it was felt that it was
important to have links into informal friendship networks if agencies
really wanted to get positive messages across. The comment was
made that a black volunteer enjoying his or her placement would
advertise a project better than a mass leafleting exercise. Door
knocking was considered more effective than paper pushing. As an
Asian member of the Group put it: 'I'm glad to see leaflets in different

languages, but they are only a means to an end. A friendly face is the same in any culture.' Getting a positive message across is vital.

To be a volunteer costs money. That is why volunteering is biased towards the middle class. A factor inhibiting volunteer involvement for the black volunteers is concern over the costs of volunteering – the expenses of being involved (fares, for example), and fears over loss of welfare benefits if expenses were claimed from the volunteer-using agency. The report recommends that agencies should do their best to ensure that expenses are provided and that, where appropriate, volunteers are well briefed on the effects on their welfare benefits.

Encouraging Black Volunteering: the Work of the National Coalition for Black Volunteering

The survey was published in 1988. It aroused considerable debate, and saw the creation of a new national organisation, the National Coalition for Black Volunteering. The Coalition seeks to promote black volunteering with demonstration projects to disseminate good practice and with training, information and advice. The Coalition is open to white and black individuals and to any volunteer-using organisation. In 1990 it was successful in obtaining grant aid from the Home Office to set up a Resource Unit. In this venture, the Coalition is working in partnership with The Volunteer Centre UK.[5]

A Text from a Training Course

When people talk about 'good practice' much gets lost in grand words, and when good practice in equal opportunities is talked about, hyperbole and rhetoric are the order of the day. However, there are practical steps to be taken.[6] To show how a volunteering agency can begin to adopt a positive equal opportunity approach, I reproduce a text from a training course undertaken by the Coalition with Westminster Volunteer Bureau.

Before setting out to recruit volunteers it is important to list out what the recruitment is for: for instance (a) what the volunteer(s) are to do, (b) which volunteer is suitable to do what type of job, (c) the length of time you want the volunteer for, (d) the out-of-pocket expenses to give the volunteer. Because you are searching for people who will perform certain tasks to provide services, it is crucial to be very careful who to recruit. It is important to stress to the people whose duty it is to recruit volunteers to be aware of the many factors that could impede or boost their efforts. Some of these are:

Commitment: in some cases, all efforts to recruit black volunteers may fail to yield results, that should not stop you trying again. Write to contacts telling them that you would like to go and visit them. If they do not reply, follow this up by telephoning them to find out if there are problems. Show them that you really want their help. Also make them feel their help would be vital to the organisation and would be very much appreciated.

Formal qualifications: do not stress formal qualifications unless they are really necessary for the work concerned. Good Equal Opportunities practice includes accepting capable people who do not have formal qualifications, and providing them with the necessary training.

Perceptions: be aware of differences in perception during interviews. Pre-conceptions may obscure the qualities and abilities of the candidates. Allocate time for the interviewee and the interviewer to ask questions of each other. This will demonstrate mutual respect in an atmosphere of good will.

Marginalisation: the cultural values of others' backgrounds should always be respected. The chances of marginalising others' traditions due to ignorance and insensitivity should be avoided by all means. Let me give an example. Talking exclusively to *The Voice*, Judge James Pickles – one is reluctant to quote him but he does make a relevant point here – revealed that he has never spoken to a 'dread' outside the dock, and confessed that his limited views could lead them to be unfairly treated. He said: 'A Rastafarian standing in front of you with dreadlocks can look rather intimidating. If we could understand their minds better, we might be able to better understand what they are doing and why they are doing it. There is no deliberate racism but there may be unconscious bias because we don't know enough about the people.' The outspoken judge added that the government should introduce race awareness training for all his colleagues.

Sensitivity: generally, there is no special formula for recruiting black volunteers. Nevertheless, there are some sensitive issues that must be taken into account. For instance, Muslim women may feel more at ease with fellow Muslim sisters. Also many blacks, both men and women, will feel more at ease if they know that there are some black people in the panel of recruiters; on the committee; serving as paid staff; or, importantly, involved amongst the volunteers. If there are, let them know; that will encourage them and give them the feeling that they are not recruited because there is a need to have a black face for the good image of the organisation. There are often cases when black people are recruited by some organisations as tokens only. Tokenism is patronising and insulting and is not a way forward to increasing black representation.

Language difficulties: should neither be ignored nor be taken as an insurmountable problem. Be prepared to recruit someone who understands some minority languages. If necessary, the organisation should be prepared to pay fees for translating and interpreting.

Time, cost, domestic work, families, housing type and place of work: are all major factors that are likely to have great effects on the possibilities to volunteer. Because many black people in this country have problems about housing or finding jobs commensurate with their qualifications and abilities, they may not be available for volunteering most of the time. That is the more reason why they should be visited at home to see if they have problems that prevent them from volunteering in their spare time – if they have spare time at all. Find out also if there are possibilities for them to do work at their home instead – stuffing envelopes, for example. All possible opportunities to employ their services should be explored and utilised. Take another example, British Telecom can arrange for calls to be transferred, so that volunteers can provide a telephone answering service from home.

It is very important that, before people are accepted as volunteers, they must be told what they are expected to do. These are the things you are going to use to attract or entice them with. The interview must not be too rigorous and tedious. Recruitment is not easy. It can sometimes be a very laborious and hard process. Every new recruit should be given the opportunity to improve or learn new skills. After the recruitment is completed, a pro-gramme of training must be established. The training should

provide volunteers with opportunities to acquire all the basic
skills or qualifications in their respective jobs for better prospects
for the future and to give them confidence, and a sense of
achievement too.

Is Equal Opportunity Policy Working?

There are encouraging signs that discrimination is breaking down.
But the statistics still tell a dismal story and, sadly, incidents of racial
prejudice and harassment are still too prevalent in 1990s Britain.
More agencies than ever *are* adopting equal opportunities policies.
That is good. But adopting policy is one thing; making it work is
another. Let me cite two examples.

As reported in the *Observer*, 1 August 1990, the Commission for
Racial Equality (CRE), after three years of relentless campaigning,
has now forced the Home Office to revamp the police entrance test so
that it will grant black people greater equality of opportunity. The
CRE argued: 'We told the Home Office that ethnic minorities may be
less likely to pass than indigenous whites because it requires a
knowledge about English phraseology not so understandable to
those not born, or wholly educated, in this country.' This is the case
even when we have long been made to believe that the Metropolitan
Police Force is an equal opportunities employer.

A recent report commissioned by the National Coalition for Black
Volunteering and The Volunteer Centre UK, showed that of a sample
of voluntary agencies, 70 per cent had equal opportunities polices.[7]
However, only 57 per cent had any black involvement (either staff,
volunteers, or management committees). Revealingly, the research
was entitled *Encouraging Signs?*, with a question mark after the title,
because while the feedback from most organisations was that they
were trying to be proactive in reaching out to the black community,
nearly a fifth of the sample took the view that the involvement of
black people was not really an issue. 'We don't see them, therefore it
doesn't matter', seemed to be the message.

Voluntary agencies must ensure that when they take on equal
opportunities they do not bow to society's prejudices. It is not
surprising that many black people regard equal opportunities as '25
years of hypocrisy'. Who can blame them? But another message is
being put over. The word 'black' is still associated with failure and
negativity.

Threats to Black Voluntary Action

Earlier, I referred to the big growth in black voluntary action, but black voluntary action is under threat. Black groups have always found it difficult to obtain funding; increased financial constraints on local government is making resources even more difficult to get. Needs are growing with unemployment on the rise again and inflation biting into those on low incomes.

To add to these problems are the adjustments to Section 11 funding. Section 11, launched in 1966, provides local authorities with additional monies to support services for black communities as defined by reference to Commonwealth status. The funding is administered by the Home Office.

Recent changes mean that some of the money earmarked for this budget will now be channelled through the new, non-elected, Training Enterprise Councils (TECs).[8] The TEC criteria is 'training and enterprise'. This means that groups which deal with social welfare (including immigration advice and interpretation, and housing) will not be eligible. Further, while TECs can fund *any* ethnic minority, projects sponsored by local authorities are still restricted to Commonwealth status. An opportunity to extend Section 11 was thus missed. Although the Home Office guidelines talk much of consultation, there is scant reference to the role, function and development of black-managed projects. There is also scant reference to volunteering. Yet this is the same Home Office which in its major review of the voluntary sector, published in 1990 and before the revisions in Section 11, recommended that volunteering for people with mixed backgrounds should be encouraged.[9]

Conclusion

It is premature to conclude that, with the advent of black volunteering in this country, racism will be eradicated. Nevertheless, it is desirable to use all possible means to eliminate racism and to introduce fairness and justice throughout society so that every member is afforded equal opportunity, regardless of the colour of their skin. At some time in our lives, every one needs the help and support of others. Voluntary action is about help. Helping one another is a virtue of humanity which transcends cultural or ethnic backgrounds. In the voluntary sector, in volunteering, the delivery of help should not be dictated or determined by the colour of people's skin.

Now that there is a crisis in volunteering, with many organisations finding it difficult to attract volunteers, it is time that black people are encouraged to take an active role. Presently, black people are massively under-represented within the voluntary sector – both as paid staff and volunteers – and services to black communities still rely on the 'good will' of white-run voluntary agencies. Since the provision of high-quality services is not exclusively the preserve of these mainstream organisations, it is only appropriate to enter into partnership with black organisations as both enablers and providers of quality service. The development of responsibilities to black voluntary organisations will empower black people by involving them in decision-making and giving them a vital role in redistributing services to meet the needs of the community as a whole – black and white.

At the moment, black people are relegated to the position of second-class citizens with no role to play in either the welfare of the people or in the economic life of the country. In order to redress and improve the situation of black people, it is important to fund black voluntary organisations which are more accessible to the black communities and are closer to the people at the grass-roots who need help. Such organisations are certainly less bureaucratic. At the same time, black participation in white organisations must be encouraged and achieved. These are the challenges for the 1990s and beyond; nothing less will do.

It may be true that 'patience, dedication and ingenuity are the stock-in-trade of volunteering', nevertheless, there are limits to that patience – black people want changes in the British system now.

CHAPTER 8

VOLUNTEERS AS ADVOCATES: SOME PERSPECTIVES FOR THE 1990s

Elaine Willis

'Who Will Advocate on My Behalf?'

Today there are people who are unable to exercise their rights as citizens as a result of the processes of marginalisation which affect their lives. There are yet others in our communities who are unable to have access to resources or faciles which they need in order to live adequately. To ignore these facts can only perpetuate a situation of increasing dissonance. In this chapter, I put forward some views as to the ways in which volunteers acting as advocates can have a crucial role to play in minimising the divisive and destructive effects of this marginalisation.

In the 1990s, there will be opportunities for voluntary activity to contribute in either one of two ways: one, by maintaining the marginalised position of some groups or individuals; or two, by acting as a means for those who are marginalised to exercise some influence over the systems which affect their lives. It is no longer possible to assume that voluntary activity, per se, makes a contribution to the lives of those who are the object of such activity. Much that has been written about the role of the welfare state and its inadequacy in providing for, and meeting, the needs of those whom it was designed to serve can also be applied to voluntary activity. Much service provision provided by volunteers, particularly in the areas of health and personal social services, has been complementary to the state service, serving needs as defined by national and local government. As a result, those who have benefited from voluntary effort have had little choice about the nature of the service they have received.

It is time to take stock of the assumed virtues of voluntary effort and to be critical of its role, particularly in providing an effective strategy against the marginalisation of some groups and individuals in our society today. I want to suggest that voluntary action by individual citizens does not consist of integrating others into society but of allowing them to choose to integrate if they so wish. In this way, voluntary activity becomes qualitatively different in its aspiration. Volunteers who act with this desire in mind perform quite a different role to that of service providers.

Before examining the reasons for the recent growth of advocacy work, it is worth considering the pathways that lead to the marginalisation of groups or individuals. It is not coincidental that the language of marginalisation has developed within the same period as advocacy work itself. It describes the ways in which people are excluded from having access to what society has to give, including income, political power, mobility, paid employment and cultural recognition. Advocacy work could be described as that activity which strives to redress the balance, that is, for individuals to have access to these things if that is their wish. The main pathways to marginalisation can be described as follows:

- the deprivation of material resources
- the lack of the physical or mental attributes of so-called 'normality'
- the admission to total institutions such as long-stay hospitals or prisons which, in turn, produces social segregation, dependency and desocialisation
- the social stigmas inflicted on individuals or groups who are perceived to be 'different', by means of stereotyping, prejudice and discrimination
- the fact of living in isolated geographical areas which are socially and economically disadvantaged

It is the recognition of these pathways which has provided the fuel for the development of advocacy work.

The Development of Advocacy Work in the UK

There has been a steady growth in the advocacy movement over the past 25 years in the UK. Recent growth can be attributed to four main causes. Firstly, there has been a rediscovery of poverty and a fresh examination of its maintenance and effect on groups and individuals. Secondly, practices and developments within the professions have created a change in relationships between the state and the people, and between professionals and their clients. Thirdly, the growth in consumerism (see pages 147–8) has created new demands by consumers on those who provide. And, fourthly, organisational changes have taken place, particularly in the public sector, in the administrative structures which provide for those in need.

These causes of the growth in advocacy have shaped the nature of advocacy itself. We are now accustomed to lobby and pressure groups advocating 'on behalf of'; take, for example, environmental groups such as Greenpeace, or housing campaigns such as those run by Shelter.

Advocacy work with individuals, on the other hand, has been less obvious but it has been critical in the recent growth of advocacy. The work that has been accomplished by those who advocate in the area of welfare rights, for example, has brought benefits both to the individuals whose case has been brought forward and, in some instances, to others where a case has highlighted a particular need for reform.

Another factor which has brought the advocacy role to the fore in recent years, has been the growth in the number and range of self-help groups, so much so that they now have a formalised network. In particular, there has been an interest on the part of many self-help groups in the process of self-advocacy – a form of advocacy which I shall describe in more detail later. Another critical factor has been the development of lay advocacy schemes and the transfer of the advocacy role from the paid professional to the unpaid volunteer advocate. The best examples of such schemes relate to work in the mental health field and, to date, these form the basis of much current thinking about advocacy work in the UK.

Current Perspectives in Advocacy Work

To enable voluntary advocacy work to be effective, there has to be a well-defined relationship between the volunteer advocate, the person or partner experiencing marginalisation, and the paid professional worker, so that the structures and relationships which generate exclusion can be challenged. There exists a number of perspectives about this relationship and here I shall outline four of them.

The Mental Health Perspective

This perspective is best described in the words of William Bingley, the legal director at MIND:

> The provision of certain basic, universal requirements is essential if individuals are to attain maximum autonomy. These include adequate diet, accommodation, income and access to the information necessary to make informed choices in exercising life options. These basic needs apply to all people regardless of age, sex, sexual orientation, handicap or political persuasion. Traditionally, professionals in the mental health care field have not seen the achievement of these objectives as central to their task. Advocacy is a response to this deficiency. It is classically defined as the process of pleading the cause of or acting on behalf of another person.[1]

The Liberation Movement Perspective

The liberation movements of the late 1960s and early 1970s in the United States and elsewhere put an increased emphasis on the rights of the individual to participation in his or her community, whatever the individual's personal characteristics. The civil rights movement, then the women's and gay liberation movements, all developed distinctive styles of laying claims to resources and entry to power bases at local and governmental levels. In this perspective, difference is celebrated as a positive attribute which contributes to the whole of society; to be black or a woman, to be gay or disabled, is claimed as the basis on which to be included, not excluded. The experience of those who are excluded is seen as the point of departure on which to build strong, active and participative lives rather than subordinated and passive ones.

The activities of these movements involve a large element of self-help and voluntary effort and, in many instances, their work has been endorsed by legislative and other reforms.

The Consumerist Perspective

Consumerism represents the purchase power of those in receipt of services which can effect change in the shape and delivery of those services. In the mid-1960s, Ralph Nader wrote his seminal texts on consumerism and, by 1973, he had spelt out clear strategies about how the consumer movement should work. He argued that the task of the consumer movement was to gather, analyse and disseminate information by demanding it and by mounting private actions by consumer groups to publicise it.

He saw the burden of this work as falling on full-time professional citizens who, as part of their role, could 'mobilise and encourage part-time citizen acitivity'. Since the early 1970s, user groups have developed the notion that individual consumers have the right to comment on the ways in which a monopoly service provider, such as the National Health Service, organises its activities when they are not considered to be in the best interest of the consumer. Equally, user groups have challenged the basic beliefs and definitions on which services for the consumer are based. For example, women's health groups have stated the view that 'mental health' is defined by white, middle-class males who bring their views to bear on the acceptable norm of mental health which excludes women's experiences.

The Professional Worker's Perspective

Social and health workers, teachers and others are undergoing a crisis of confidence about their work methods and goals. It was hoped that institutional reform would lead to individual improvement and that attention to the individual would develop more human institutions. Often, this aspiration has not been realised and professional workers have been searching out more satisfactory and participatory ways of achieving their goals. Advocacy is perceived to be one such way, even though effective advocacy can challenge the needs and goals of organisations and institutions to which professional workers belong and in whose interests they act.

Models of Advocacy

Given that there are these different perspectives on advocacy, it is nevertheless possible to distinguish three models of advocacy which are influencing current practices – those of paid advocacy, self-advocacy and citizen advocacy.

Paid Advocacy

A number of people undertake advocacy as part of their paid employment. Such people are described as paid 'voluntary' advocates because they have chosen to interpret the advocate role as part of their job definition where others in the same job have not. Such paid advocates are limited to specific occupations where there is relative freedom, and where there is the possibility of setting time aside for the detailed work. Legal advocacy is perhaps the best-known form of paid advocacy, particularly in the areas of legal and welfare rights advice. But, increasingly, a number of voluntary organisations are employing people in a paid capacity to take on the advocate role.

Self-Advocacy

This model of advocacy might be said to be the true goal of all advocacy work. Here, volunteer advocate and partner are one, and the individual both speaks out on his or her own behalf and takes action to remedy the complaint. Self-advocacy can be described as 'the act of making choices and decisions and bringing about the desired change for oneself'.[2]

There are various models of self-advocacy being employed at present, each with their own advantages and disadvantages. Here I shall describe four models, those described as autonomous or ideal, divisional, coalition, and service provider system.

Autonomous or ideal model

In this model, the self-advocacy function is carried out entirely separately from the professional service provider, often with the assistance of an independent adviser. For example, people may gather together under the umbrella of a local voluntary organisation, such as a MIND or Age Concern group, and together lobby for change in the way that a locally provided service is run.

The advantage of this model is that there cannot be any direct conflict of interest between the advocacy and the service function because the two are entirely separate from each other. Those who advocate on behalf of their own needs are likely to be more effective because of their identification with the demands being put forward in an advocacy context. The main disadvantage is that the advocacy function has to be entirely self-supporting and this may require access to a greater level of resources to be truly effective than the self-advocates are able to provide.

Divisional model
This model offers more resources, but can lead to a conflict of interest. It enables people to act as independent advocates, but within the professional service or parent organisation. Because of this, those who are advocates are able to draw on the resources of the parent body and have the opportunity to make a greater impact on the system which they are asking to be changed or reformed. For example, a voluntary services co-ordinator within a hospital may set up an independent advocacy scheme with residents which the hospital is prepared to fund and support, but over which it does not seek control.

The main disadvantage is the increased potential for a conflict of interest between the advocate and the service provider.

Coalition model
Sometimes a self-advocacy group is formed by people with different interests or abilities. Whether formed under the autonomous or divisional model, there are obvious advantages to such a group. These include the ability of the self-advocacy group to generate resources for its activities and the potential for increased political power when dealing with the professional service provider concerned. The main weakness of this model, which may not emerge until the group has been formed for a little while, is that its more able members may dominate the others, or that the least able may restrict the group's ability to act as an advocate. In either case, the inability of the group to maintain its role as an advocate on behalf of all its members will inevitably weaken its self-advocacy function.

Service provider model
This advocacy model mirrors the service provision functions that a scheme or group may advocate against. Here, the service provider or parent organisation establishes a self-advocacy group as part of its own system. It is perhaps the easiest model to establish because it allows for adequate resources to be provided and easy access to the system by the self-advocacy group. However, the self-advocacy function is weakest because the potential for a conflict of interest is strongest and, in time, the group may simply become a token gesture towards self-advocacy.

While these models have been most clearly identified within the

advocacy work of those with learning difficulties, there is no reason why they should not be applied to other areas, too. The most important characteristic of self-advocacy is that the interests and concerns of advocate and partner are one. This is not the case in citizen advocacy, and it is here that the role of the volunteer advocate becomes most contentious and, arguably, the most difficult to perform.

Citizen Advocacy

Citizen advocacy is where a citizen who is unpaid and independent of human services creates a relationship with a person who is at risk of social exclusion. Such a citizen chooses to understand, respond to and represent that person's interests as if they were the advocate's own, thus bringing their partner's gifts and concerns into the circles of ordinary community life.

There are a number of citizen advocacy schemes or projects being established, all of which are at different stages of development. There is no 'ideal' scheme, but more a plurality of schemes which are evolving to meet the needs and personalities of the partners involved and their volunteer advocates. Some schemes employ a co-ordinator whose role is to enable partners and volunteer advocates to walk a 'path of citizen advocacy'. This phrase has been coined by the Sheffield Advocacy Project and it is worth describing this path, which has seven steps, in some detail.[3]

Step one:
Seeking out people with disabilities who are: lonely, isolated, excluded, in danger, desperate, poor, denied services, lack opportunities and hope.

Step two:
Inviting members of the community to become involved with a disabled/excluded person as a volunteer advocate: to become friends with, speak up on behalf of, represent, include and to seek out opportunities for them.

Step three:
Introducing the advocate and partner to each other; spending time together, to get to know one another; respecting each other.

Step four:
Helping the advocate understand their partner's situation by

introducing the principles of citizen advocacy, describing their partner's situation, looking at possible directions and options for now and the future together with their partner.

Step five:
Giving back-up and support to the advocate through providing information, meeting, talking and listening.

Step six:
Developing contacts to help in the recruitment of advocates and using existing advocates to identify others who may become involved.

Step seven:
Balancing activities and tasks through evaluation and reviews, discussion and flexibility.

Volunteers who act as citizen advocates are recruited to perform a role which requires them to act in accordance with the values of their partner. The role of the scheme co-ordinator is to offer support to both and to be clear about the principles which the 'path' seeks to express.

The Purpose of Advocacy

Having described in some detail the activity of advocacy, it is important to look at the purpose of advocacy. One established and well-tried function of advocacy is the settlement of individual disputes by representation. There may be formal machinery in place, such as that provided by an industrial tribunal, which provides a framework for the advocate to put the case for resolving a particular dispute. A second function of advocacy is to promote the partici-pation of those who are excluded, within the terms which they themselves define and desire. A third function of advocacy is an indirect one, in that the settlement of disputes may place an additional pressure upon systems which may result in a change of policy on the part of the service provider concerned. The role of the advocate becomes more important in a climate such as that currently evolving, where government is distancing itself from decision-making in particular spheres and relying more on intermediaries to make judgements. As the 'patient', 'prisoner', or 'benefit recipient' becomes treated more as a consumer of services than a passive recipient of them, this, too, will create a greater demand for the role of the advocate.

Advocacy has a befriending function, but while the role of befriender and advocate overlap, they also differ in important ways. Both advocates and befrienders spend time and share activities with their partners. They will both learn to communicate with their partner and understand what is important to them. Advocates, however, have additional tasks which involve acting on behalf of their partners and in their best interests to ensure that their needs are being met and their rights protected. The advocate's primary commitment and loyalty is to his or her partner and not to the service or service provider. This is why befrienders often appear to be more acceptable to service providers because, unlike advocates, they are not seen to get 'over-involved', to question too much, or to interfere with the service provider's decisions.

Advocacy as a Form of Voluntary Activity

Advocacy, as a form of voluntary activity, has an important role to play as we reach the end of the twentieth century. Advocates can be effective in ways that professional workers often cannot be, but, as with other forms of voluntary activity, advocacy has the potential to create a new dependency on the part of the individual. Some forms of advocacy may end up reinforcing the *status quo* in relation to systems and institutions rather than fulfilling its radical potential. There is a danger that some people may say that if advocacy changes the world, even in part, for one person, then the world has changed – and in a certain sense this is true. However, if advocacy work in the long term does nothing to try to effect change in relation to the organisational structures and processes which prevent individuals' participation, then it only goes part way towards achieving its ends. In acting on behalf of their partners, advocacy schemes are gathering vital information on issues of our time which, if kept 'hidden', will do nothing to tackle the identification of those things which exclude individuals and work against their voice being heard.

Another aspect to bear in mind is that of the relationship of advocacy to other forms of voluntary activity. The potential for conflict exists not only between an advocate and a service provider, but between an advocate and another volunteer acting on behalf of the service provider. Those whose job it is to organise or co-ordinate volunteer activity in any given area may find themselves having to deal with this issue and having to find ways of resolving or managing different approaches to similar problems.

A major challenge facing advocacy schemes concerns the recruitment of advocates. In this respect, it is no different from other forms of voluntary activity. Who are we looking for to be volunteer advocates? In certain forms, advocacy work is looking for educated, knowledgeable and professional people. This raises the problem which occurs in other forms of volunteering, namely, that recruitment takes place from among restricted parts of the population. Although such people may have influence within their own communities, they do not always have the kind of attitude which is favourable to developing the advocate relationship, or pursuing lobbying or representative activities. To pursue such a narrow recruitment policy may, in the long term, simply serve to absorb advocacy work into the professionalised world and thus lose its credibility to develop a different form of helping and mutual partnership. This leads me to the conclusion that the self-advocacy model remains the most potent one for change.

CHAPTER 9

SELF-HELP GROUPS: IS THERE ROOM FOR VOLUNTEERS?

Mai Wann

Introduction

Self-help and mutual-aid groups are by no means a new idea. There has been, however, a recent mushrooming of groups formed around an illness or social condition. Attempts to count them and to produce a complete register of self-help groups, both local and national, have only been partially successful. Groups come and go depending on the needs and energies of their members. Furthermore, many groups are informal and do not wish to appear in a directory. Any estimate of the number of self-help groups in Britain is therefore likely to be inaccurate.

We can form a rough idea, however, of the breadth of the movement by looking at a number of local directories of self-help groups published by councils for voluntary service and other self-help support centres. For instance, the Rugby *Directory of Self-Help and Carers Groups* (May 1989) lists 41 groups; the *Directory of Self-Help in Nottingham and District* lists 150 groups; the *Leicester Self-Help Directory in Health and Social Welfare* (1989) lists 159 groups; and the *Directory of Self-Help Groups in Thamesdown* (1989) lists 86 groups.

Another way of listing self-help groups is by special interest. National specialist organisations keep a register of the groups they support. For example, *Cancerlink* directory (1989) lists a total of 324 cancer support groups up and down the country. And Alzheimer's Disease Society has 110 groups on their database (1990).

Finally, Help for Health – an information service for health care staff and consumers based at Southampton – maintains a database of national self-help groups amounting to 1,049 groups (1990).

Within the last 10 years, self-help groups have been making their voices heard. The voluntary sector has responded positively to requests for support, information and practical help, both nationally and on a local level. Councils for voluntary service have started employing workers with a brief to help develop self-help groups in the areas of health and social welfare. Nottingham CVS set up a self-help support service in 1982. It was followed by Leicester CVS, which appointed a worker in response to enquiries and requests for help from self-help groups in 1983.

A real boost to self-help support locally was given by the DHSS-funded programme, the Self-Help Alliance (1986–89), which consisted of 18 local projects. They explored different ways of supporting a wide range of self-help groups. Detailed descriptions and an evaluation of their work have been published by the Tavistock Institute of Human Relations as part of their Occasional Papers series (1988–89).

With such an upsurge in self-help activity there is clearly a need to share information and learn from each other's experiences. The National Self-Help Support Centre (NSHSC) was set up in 1986 to encourage support to self-help groups in the fields of health and social services and to focus national attention on the need for such support. NSHSC has been successful in developing networks of people involved in supporting groups, both through specialist organisations on a national level and locally in a generalist way. Three networks meet every year: the local self-help support workers' network, the self-help organisations' network and the network of black and ethnic minority workers.

A quarterly bulletin, *Mutual Aid and Self-Help (MASH)*, is produced by NSHSC and is mailed to over 1,000 groups, voluntary agencies and individuals involved in supporting groups. Conferences, seminars and training courses are also organised by NSHSC to encourage the dialogue between professionals and groups and to familiarise newcomers in the field with issues and practicalities relevant to supporting self-help groups.

In 1989 NSHSC was given funds by the Department of Health to continue acting as a reference point for self-help support nationally.

How Self-Help Groups Came About

Self-help and mutual-aid groups are made up of people who have a common problem or concern and get together to do something about it. Typically, groups are formed around a physical or mental illness, such as the Herpes Association; or a dependency, such as the Women and Tranquillisers Group; or a life crisis, such as the Foundation for the Study of Infant Deaths; or a state which may be stigmatised by society, such as Gingerbread – an organisation for lone parents. There are also groups formed by people who look after a relative or friend with a disability or severe illness, such as the Alzheimer's Disease Society. These groups are better known as carers' support groups.

Generally speaking, self-help groups exist where there are problems of isolation or where people feel marginalised. The decision to belong to a self-help group arises not only from the disability itself and the need for information and practical advice, but also from a wish not to be labelled as 'the disabled person'. When every woman in a group has had a mastectomy, one cannot be singled out as 'the woman with the mastectomy'.

In cases where the disability or illness are not immediately visible, the pressure to be among people who feel the same is even greater. Phobias, depression, parenting and dependencies are common issues for self-help groups.

People who form or join a self-help group are usually looking for support, information, practical help and advice. They wish to give as well as receive. Talking about their problems and their ways of coping and listening to other people's experiences help them to clarify their own thoughts and perceptions. Members of a self-help group seek to lighten their burden by sharing with others in a similar position – 'a problem shared is a problem halved'.

Issues in Self-Help

Before discussing the value of self-help and the contribution which groups make to their members, and the health and social services in general, it is important to note that, however many success stories we come across, there will always be people who are disappointed by self-help groups. There will also be those who do not wish to join a group because they do not want to share others' problems in addition to coping with their own.

A study of Contact-a-Family (CaF),[1] an organisation for parents with children with disabilities, identified some of the reasons why people do not join a group, and some of the disappointments resulting from joining groups. Many parents who are approached by CaF, or who express an initial interest in the organisation's activities, are quite happy to receive the newsletter and to have no further involvement. There are also parents who become members and participate in some activities, but their level of involvement remains low. Some have no specific expectations. As one of the parents said: 'I just went along out of interest. Tracey was much younger then and we did not have any particular problems.'

In other cases, the experience may be quite negative: 'I just felt as if I didn't belong. I didn't know anybody there.' This particular parent went on to participate more fully in the group and eventually got something out of it. For many parents, however, the decision to join involves more than just taking out a membership, as the researchers explain:

> Joining a voluntary organisation is often an act of very limited significance. The new member may simply be contributing to a good cause or gaining access to the news and information provided in a magazine. But in the case of a self-help group the decision to join may have much greater significance, for it involves acknowledgement by the joiner that he or she has the problem with which the group is concerned, and this raises what may be deep-seated questions about the joiner's identity. Thus in the case of CaF it requires recognition that the joiner's child is handicapped and the decision to become, at least in some degree, part of the handicapped world. These may be large steps to take psychologically . . . For these reasons members' feelings about belonging to CaF are more than simply a set of attitudes like those which are commonly examined in surveys of public opinion. Rather, at any rate for some members, they relate to a process of personal change and to the development of mutually supportive relationships. Moreover, members' problems and those of their children are not static: as they change so may involvement in CaF.

Reluctance to join a group may also come for reasons outside the individual. For some black and ethnic minority people, the question is not so much whether or not they accept their own problem but what can a white group or organisation offer them? Will they feel comfortable enough in a white group to give and take support? The Black Carers Support Group in Lozells, Birmingham is very clear about the reasons for initiating a group specifically for Afro-Caribbean carers. Avril Wiltshire, a district nurse in Handsworth, explained:

> We started a group called the Black Carers Group in January 1989. And this came about because we, as professionals, visited some consultation meetings which were held by the Special Action Project. After sitting through these meetings for carers we realised that there weren't many black people there and knowing the size of the black population in the community we knew that something was actually wrong . . . Being a district nurse I was in touch with many carers. I started asking them whether they would find it useful to come to a group and they all said 'yes'. . . . We formed a group at the Annie Wood Centre. Why a separate group? Professionals also asked us the same question, adding that 'they are all the same people'. Well, they are not. They may have the same problems, but there are differences. For instance, most black people felt more relaxed in their own environment. There was no racism among themselves. They were able to communicate in their own patois. The steering group, on the other hand, includes white workers and this has been discussed by the group who find it absolutely fine. . . . There is also a mixed group for carers at the Annie Wood Centre. Those black carers who prefer to go to the mixed group can do that. So they have a choice. The Black Carers Group will remain exclusively for black carers as long as there are black carers who need it.

A Role for Volunteers?

The need to be among people who have the same problem and who express it in similar ways is an essential part of a self-help group. This is what brings people together in the first place and what keeps them in the group. Most groups, however, find it useful to invite volunteers to their steering committee or management group. The Black Carers Support Group is no exception. The carers are very clear about the need for a steering group which is made up of people other than themselves. They find that their lives are heavily loaded with duties and they cannot take on any more. Furthermore, the steering group is most useful when it includes people with particular expertise, access to information, and skills for organising and fund-raising.

Self-help groups do not automatically give their members all they need. The trust and confidence that are necessary for any group to function need building up. A lot of hard work is required in organising a meeting, preparing publicity about the group, and raising money to finance the group's activities. Many self-help groups find that they need support from outside their membership. Their needs are often met by professionals in the health and social work fields, as well as by voluntary sector workers and volunteers.

The role of paid or unpaid supporters varies from group to group but, on the whole, they become a link between the group and the service providers, lending it their credibility and knowledge of the system. While it is common for a group to need outside help for at least some time until its members feel able to tackle every issue on their own, it is important for the skills and information to be transferred from the supporter to the members of the group in a sensitive way. This process is often described today as facilitating or empowering groups.

Self-Help and Mutual Aid: A Long History

Self-help and mutual aid, however, have a long history. The two terms originate from opposing ideologies. Self-help, a term attributed to Samuel Smiles,[2] a nineteenth-century economist and moralist, comprises self-reliance, 'standing on one's own two feet' and being able to cope and succeed through one's own efforts. According to Kropotkin, on the other hand, mutual aid has its roots in collectivism – a system within which people protect each other from exploitation because they have shared interests.[3]

For Smiles, the emphasis was on individuals being responsible for themselves and not relying on the state. Kropotkin, on the other hand, stressed the other side of the concept. He spoke as an anarchist and atheist, rejecting the formal discipline and hierarchy which government imposes as a condition of central or local state aid. He also rejected the role of religion and the churches which preach charity thereby conferring superiority on the giver. For Kropotkin, mutual aid is a natural human force which binds people together; co-operative endeavour is the essence.[4]

While the ambiguity between the two remains – according to some critics of self-help, such as Gareth H. Williams[5] who argues that 'modern self-help organisations are the progeny of an uneasy relationship between two ideologies: individualism and collectivism,' – in practice, these two rather purist forms of action have come closer together. Self-help leads to self-development through association with others, while mutual aid recognises the need to develop one's own skills and abilities as well as to protect others.

Empowerment

The term 'empowerment', which is in current use, encompasses both activities and aims to help the individual develop his or her own strength through sharing, trusting, learning and taking collective action. This is particularly true of mental health groups whose very purpose is to help their members come out of a position of powerlessness.

Gael Lindenfield,[6] a psychotherapist and groupwork consultant, who initiated Mind Your Self, a mental health project in Leeds, identified the problems of people joining mental health groups and produced the following list: 'Low self-esteem; lack of assertiveness; poor communication skills; lack of spontaneity; lack of physical energy; inability to trust; inability to take risks; no goals or sense of direction . . . Stress and lack of social support contribute in accentuating these problems and may cause mental illness.' Through well-supported self-help groups, she argues, people can develop relationships and improve the quality of their lives. The support offered by Mind Your Self includes:

Self-help groups led by either a professional worker or an experienced volunteer – usually a client who has progressed forward and taken some training in counselling.
Courses and workshops led by experienced qualified therapists and counsellors e.g. assertiveness training; coping with stress; coping with anger; confidence building; transactional analysis.
Individual counselling service.

Gael Lindenfield argues that:

Empowering people means being prepared to demystify the skills of helping. People who come to the project for help have the opportunity to learn group work and counselling. In the short-term, this may need considerable investment in staff resources. It may also appear as contrary to the character of self-help when the staff take an active role in leading the groups and offering complementary therapy.

From her own experience, however, she concludes that 'the risk of becoming more involved in the groups has paid off because the self-help side of the project has grown amazingly strong. There is a network of hundreds of people who give effective, informal support to each other and many others who have acquired more sophisticated helping skills.'

A similar need for long-term support is felt by women's groups. The aim of many women's groups is self-development and empowerment through participation in a self-help and mutual-aid group. Self-help groups seek to restore women's sense of autonomy over their own lives, to give women self-reliance and to lessen their dependency on institutions that define their lives. The example of the Women and Tranquillisers Group based at Womankind in Bristol – a project which received funding from the Department of Health during 1986–89 under the umbrella of the Self-help Alliance, and is now run by volunteers, illustrates how individual women can be helped through participating in a group. The following description is given by Julia Warren and Joyce Walls,[7] members of the Women and Tranquillisers Group.

We are two women who came together through a women and mental health self-help project in Bristol. Although our experiences with tranquillisers were different, we have many things in common. One of us was on many different tranquillisers for nearly 20 years, and came to the project through the tranquilliser self-help group. The other, on various pills including valium, sleeping tablets and strong pain killers, came to the project after applying for the tranx outreach post there. Now both of us are successfully running tranquilliser groups for women in the Bristol area. We have found that each group's needs are different. For example, one group may be in the centre of a town, with women from various areas, classes and background; groups set up in a community will more than likely consist of women of similar class and background. But regardless of location, the success of groups has depended on the good communication we have had in working with GPs, social workers, and other statutory and non-statutory organisations. All our groups meet weekly, the times and days being decided after consulting with the women in those areas. Women come along to the weekly meetings as and when they feel they need to. The only guidelines we strongly emphasise are that: (i) women arrive on time, as arriving late can be disruptive to the rest of the group; (ii) everything said in the group is completely confidential; (iii) no other member of the group interrupts when someone else is speaking, unless they feel that what they say will help the other person.

Each group runs two hours. In this time all women are encouraged to share with the group any feelings that are important to them. But just as the needs of groups are different so are the needs of each woman. The time taken by each member of the group will be different each week as one woman may need only 10 minutes while another who may be experiencing a crisis will need much longer. On request by the groups, we have, where possible, provided information and education, such as relaxation tapes, books and information on workshops running in the area. We have also arranged for outside speakers to talk about diet, vitamins and alternative medicine. The groups themselves have organised social events which have been financed by their own efforts in fundraising.

Our personal development has been successful because we have continued to learn and gain information through listening, good support, supervision and training from both other workers and each other. We have also gained the understanding that each person running a group does so because of what comes from inside them; trying to run a group like someone else just doesn't seem to work. Most women in the group say that they prefer the groups to be led. This is because, in their everyday life, they are the one people come to with their problems or they seem to always take control of situations and help everyone else out; people always regard them as the ones that 'can cope'. The groups give these women a chance to take time for themselves and be listened to, without having to take control and organise things.

Some women do very well in the group; they cut down and eventually come off all their tablets. Others are not ready to start cutting down but are just as much a valued member of the group. They all support each other both in and outside the meetings by keeping contact by phone or meeting outside the group. Some have gone on to setting up their own groups while still using their original group for support; others who have successfully come off all their tranquillisers will stay in the group and use their own experience to help other women. The histories and futures of all the women are many and varied. The groups can only offer so much, but we have found that the inner strength of the women as individuals and as a group, and the ability they have found in taking control of their lives, has made them grow, brought back confidence and continued to help them through the struggles in their lives.

Support in the case of the Women and Tranquillisers Group means more than offering to facilitate and organise the meetings. It means helping individual women to find jobs or training courses, or other ways of developing their skills. The resources available to the women – especially during the three years when the project was funded by the Department of Health, and the access to the facilities at the Bristol Settlement where Womankind was based – were crucial in helping them change the circumstances which had led them to their dependency in the first place.

A similar need to take control of their lives brought women with a dependency on alcohol to the Drinking to Cope Group, which was initiated by Barbara Croft in Derbyshire. Women join Drinking to Cope because they need help with sorting out their lives as well as breaking a dependency. They need support in dealing with family situations which are difficult, with changes in their own lives, with finding new challenges. One of their common concerns is the prejudice and lack of understanding which they face in the rural community where they live. Barbara Croft described how and why she initiated the group at a conference organised by the National Self-Help Support Centre in March 1990. Part of her talk is reproduced below.

Drinking to Cope, the group I started up in February 1988 in Matlock, came about because I had a 20 year battle with alcohol. Eventually, I got to see the right psychiatrist. It shocked me silly because he didn't tell me what to do. I was left with my own resources ... O.K. I stopped drinking, but life hadn't changed. I was still me with all my problems and people were still giving me a lot of hassle. So, there were two things there: first of all looking at the addiction and doing something about that and then sorting out other problems. Having come through that, I thought about other people in the area who might not have been as fortunate as I was. I had support and a good psychiatrist who put me in touch with a group called Spectrum for people with mental health problems. That was a shock! I didn't think of my problem as a mental health problem. It took me many months to accept that I did have a mental health problem . . . Having decided to initiate a group for women who had a problem with alcohol I started talking to people who might be able to help. First of all I was told there wasn't a problem in Matlock and I just went around wasting my time. When I did carry on and advertised it in the paper everybody knew I had a drink problem. Having done that I waited for all these people to flood in. Eventually I was joined by one woman. But two people are a group. And we talked and talked, having a laugh about things we have no right to laugh about. We talked about guilt and shame and what's so bad about being a woman who drinks . . . Most women who have stopped drinking and who should feel proud of their achievement are too ashamed to say 'I had a drink problem'. It says something about how we feel about ourselves as drinkers, it says much more about how we feel about ourselves as women, and it says a tremendous amount about the society we live in that criminalises a woman who drinks.[8]

Organisations which work with people with learning difficulties (a term that has replaced mental handicaps) find themselves fighting against social prejudice, too. The Campaign for People with Mental Handicaps which has recently changed its name to Values into Action (VIA), sees itself as an advocacy organisation. Steve Dowson,[9] VIA director, explains: 'Our cause is to promote the right of people with learning difficulties to become full citizens and to receive whatever support services they need to make citizenship possible.'

People with learning difficulties are segregated, placed in special day centres and given training for what they are assumed to be capable of achieving. While their opinions as service users are sometimes sought, it is more common for the service providers to make decisions on their behalf.

Currently, however, with the rapid growth of the international People First movement, new independent groups are emerging. People First groups aim to achieve self-advocacy – a group's ability to speak for itself. To get there, the groups offer their members opportunities to develop their abilities more fully. Taking on practical tasks, such as organising meetings and keeping a record of discussions, is one of the ways to help group members learn new skills. It is also a way to gain confidence both as individuals and as a group. In the longer run, it leads to autonomy which is an essential ingredient of self-help and mutual-aid groups.

However, for many groups who need to break away from dependency, marginalisation and stigma – and, in particular, for the type of group described in this chapter – autonomy is a long-term goal. In order to learn to speak for themselves, groups need advocates and supporters. But their advocates and supporters also need to learn new ways of helping people who have been disadvantaged for a long time. The traditional charitable approach of doing things for others is not helpful to self-help groups.

Supporters – whether paid workers, specialists, or volunteers – have to learn to appreciate and respect the strength and independence which members of self-help groups possess. Together, group members and supporters can identify and agree on the specific tasks that need to be carried out. In tackling them, they need to pass on skills, to impart knowledge and to share power. Being a member of a steering group, is one of the ways in which a professional can offer expertise, energy, experience and knowledge to groups without taking over control.

The Role of the Professionals

Attempts by professionals to set up groups around a particular disease or dependency, such as heart disease and smoking, are not, on the whole, successful. Groups initiated by health professionals tend to adopt the medical model of health which is disease-based. These groups usually focus quite narrowly on the particular problem. Sometimes the sheer presence of the doctor or other professional in a group reminds people that they are there to discuss the risk of heart failure or the need to give up smoking, and not their other worries.

One of the key elements of self-help groups, however, is that they reject the medical model of health and they look at the individual not as a person with a particular problem, but as a whole person with a range of problems as well as positive contributions to make. In groups initiated by lay people, members feel that they can bring a whole range of problems and experiences to the group, some of which may not relate directly to the particular disease. By discussing different aspects of their lives, people can begin to identify ways of coping and to make changes that may help them.

Medical staff and other professionals can be brought in to give a particular talk or to answer questions. These sessions are invaluable to the group who are given a chance to find out more about their illness without putting pressure on their own GP and in an environment which feels safe to them. They are not alone; they are surrounded by others with similar problems who are likely to be supportive. Furthermore, people listen to each other's questions and the replies given by the professional. In this way, they gain more information and expand their own knowledge.

In establishing a dialogue with professionals, the group also has the opportunity to discuss and make suggestions about changes in the way services are provided. This is a crucial point for many self-help groups who wish to go beyond giving support to each other and who aim to use their own experiences in order to improve the services for others. It is also a point of potential conflict between service providers and users.

In a group, people have a chance to identify and discuss more fully their health needs. They learn to communicate their collective needs and to make suggestions about improving the provision of services. This is both useful and threatening to the service providers. Professionals in the health and social services are not always confident in self-help groups. By their training they are led to believe that only they have the knowledge and expertise necessary to make decisions which affect their patients' lives. How can they accept being challenged and questioned by lay people?

Furthermore, some self-help groups, such as tranx groups, blame GPs for creating the problem by prescribing tranquillisers in the first place. How can doctors trust tranx groups? It is a real challenge for professionals to share power with the people whom they are trying to help. But when a dialogue is established and a more equal relationship develops, there are clear benefits for both sides.

By getting closer together, professionals and self-help groups can develop their trust in each other. This can help them see things from a different perspective and expand their understanding of a disease or disability. For the less-common conditions, in particular, self-help groups are a source of valuable information and knowledge. Professionals, on the other hand, can lend a group their credibility and refer new members to it.

As the examples of self-help groups outlined in this chapter illustrate, co-operation between professionals and groups can lead to successful outcomes. The Women and Tranquillisers Group works closely with GPs in order to help its members. Coming off tranquillisers requires careful supervision by a doctor, as well as support from others with the same dependency.

Drinking to Cope also found that mental health workers were a source of support and help. Similarly, a paediatrician who became closely involved with Contact-a-Family introduced a member of a local group of parents with children with disabilities as, 'Mrs X. who knows more about Downs Syndrome than I do.' Carers and people with a particular disease have an intimate knowledge of their own problems and develop ways of coping which may be useful to others. Moreover, by sharing their knowledge with professionals in the health and social services, self-help groups also aim to influence service provision.

Self-Help in the 1990s

Currently, there is great interest in user involvement in planning and organising services. Both the NHS Review, *Working for Patients* (HMSO, 1989)[10] and the White Paper, *Caring for People* (HMSO, 1989)[11] have frequent references to increasing consumer choice, and 'putting the user of services in the driving seat'. Furthermore, as an increasing number of services are likely to be contracted out to the independent sector (both voluntary and private) self-help groups may well become service providers.

For some well-established groups backed by national voluntary organisations, this is an opportunity to respond to their members' needs. Day care centres managed by carers' groups should be more sensitive and responsive to their users. Other groups, however, who have not developed formal structures and whose main aim is to provide a safe environment for mutual support may be under pressure to provide a service simply because it is not available. For instance, many Asian parents are reluctant to use respite care because they fear that their children may not feel at home in a white environment. However, the pressure to run their own centres may be too much for the more fragile groups and they need to be protected from it.

The challenge for self-help and mutual-aid groups in the 1990s is not whether or not they will continue to increase their numbers. There has been a mushrooming of groups and the signs are that, as people become more interested in their health and health care, they form more groups and organisations. The challenge is rather for groups to be allowed to differ. To date, the strength of self-help groups has been their freedom to form the structures they need; to be formal or informal; to be local or national; to be large or small; to be specialist or general; to provide support or to campaign for change; to organise social events or to share feelings.

Will the changes which are about to take place in the health and social services force self-help groups to conform to certain models? Or, are they going to find enough support to develop in their own unique ways? Perhaps one of the contributions which volunteers can make is to ensure that self-help groups remain autonomous and able to determine their own future.

Notes

Note: The Volunteer Centre became The Volunteer Centre UK in 1987. In details of publications cited below, it has been abbreviated to Volunteer Centre throughout.

Introduction

1 The Volunteer Centre survey is detailed in J. Field and B. Hedges, *A National Survey of Volunteering* (Social and Community Planning Research, 1984).
2 S. Hall, *The Voluntary Sector under Attack?* (Islington Voluntary Action Council, 1989), from which all quotes from Hall in the Introduction are taken.
3 The Volunteer Centre UK, *Charter for Volunteers: A Proposal*, Policy Discussion Document 3 (Volunteer Centre, 1983).

1 Volunteering and Society, 1960 to 1990

1 W. Beveridge, *Voluntary Action* (Allen & Unwin, 1948).
2 For example, HM(62)29, HM(69)58.
3 *Half Our Future: Report of the Central Advisory Council for England* (HMSO, 1963).
4 *Service by Youth: Report of a Committee of the Youth Service Development Council* (DES, 1966).
5 *The Place of Voluntary Service in After-Care: Second Report of the Committee Chaired by the Dowager Marchioness of Reading* (HMSO, 1967).
6 *Report of the Committee on Local Authority and Allied Personal Social Serivces* (HMSO, 1968).

7 T. Dartington, *Task Force* (Mitchell Beazley and Task Force, 1971).

8 ibid.

9 C. Allinson, *Young Volunteers?* (Community Projects Foundation, 1978).

10 *Half Our Future*, cited at note 3.

11 *Community Service and the Curriculum*, Schools Council Working Paper no. 17 (HMSO, 1968).

12 *The Voluntary Worker in the Social Services: Report of a Committee Jointly Set Up by NCSS and NISWT under the Chairmanship of Geraldine M. Aves* (Allen & Unwin, 1969).

13 *Report of the Committee on Local Authority and Allied Personal Social Services*, cited at note 6.

14 P. Baldock, 'Why community action? The historical origins of the radical trend in British community work', in *Readings in Community Work*, ed. by P. Henderson and D. N. Thomas (Allen & Unwin, 1981).

15 A. Twelvetrees, 'Whither community work?' in *Community Work in the 80s*, ed. by D. N. Thomas (NISW, 1983).

16 See, for example, *Community Involvement Resource Pack* (National Youth Bureau, 1984).

17 *Guidelines for Relationships between Volunteers and Paid Non-Professional Workers* (Volunteer Centre, 1975).

18 *Report of the Working Group on Co-operation between Volunteers and Paid Workers* (DHSS, 1979, unpublished).

19 *Health Services Management if Industrial Relations Break Down*, HC(79)20 (DHSS, 1979).

20 L. Chalker, S. Moore and A. Rowe, *We Are Richer than We Think* (Conservative Central Office, 1978).

21 At WRVS conference, January 1981.

22 P. Henderson and P. Taylor, *Voluntarism* (Association of Community Workers, 1982).

23 P. Beresford and S. Croft, *Community Control of Social Services Departments* (Battersea Community Action, 1980); R. Hadley and S. Hatch, *Social Welfare and the Failure of the State* (Allen & Unwin, 1981); F. Gladstone, *Voluntary Action in a Changing World* (Bedford Square Press, 1979); *Social Workers, their Roles and Tasks: Report of the Barclay Committee* (NISW/Bedford Square Press, 1982); I. Illich, *Disabling Professions* (Marion Boyars, 1977).

24 *A Guide to GLC Grant-Aid for Voluntary and Community Organisations* (GLC, 1982).

25 *VAS News* (April 1982).
26 C. Ball, *Twist and Shake Revisited* (Volunteer Centre, 1985).
27 *Charter for Volunteers: A Proposal*, Policy Discussion Document 3 (Volunteer Centre, 1983).
28 *Policies towards Unemployment and Volunteering* (Volunteer Centre, 1983).
29 M. Rankin, *Working in the Margin* (Volunteer Centre, 1985).
30 See, for example, J. Robertson, *Future Work* (Temple Smith/ Gower, 1985); C. Jenkins and B. Sherman, *The Collapse of Work* (Eyre Methuen, 1979).
31 R. M. Titmuss, *The Gift Relationship* (Penguin, 1973).
32 P. Gay and S. Hatch, *Voluntary Work and Unemployment* (Manpower Services Commission, 1983); I. Mocroft and M. Doyle, *Volunteers at Work* (Volunteer Centre/Centre for Research in Social Policy, 1987); K. Ford, *A Matter of Choice* (Project VBx, 1985).
33 Department of Health, *Caring for People: Community Care in the Next Decade and Beyond*, Cm 849 (HMSO, 1989).
34 *Guardian*, 20 April 1990.
35 The Rt Hon. John Patten, MP, *Active Citizenship: A New Vision for Britain in the 1990s* (Volunteer Centre, 1989).
36 Home Office, *Profiting from Partnership: Efficiency Scrutiny of Government Funding of the Voluntary Sector* (HMSO, 1990).
37 *Encouraging Citizenship: Report of the Commission on Citizenship* (HMSO, 1990).
38 *Report of the Commission on Youth and the Needs of the Nation* (privately published, 1980).
39 E. Colombatto, *Nationwide Social Service: A Proposal for the 1980s*, Centre for Labour Economics, Discussion Paper, no. 84 (LSE, 1980).
40 *Youth Call: A Debate on Youth and Service to the Community* (Youth Call, 1981).
41 *Count Us In* (Tawney Society, 1984).
42 *Youth Call*, cited at note 40.
43 *Observer*, 2 September 1990.
44 *The Promotion of Volunteering: A Value Base for Voluntary Action in the 1990s* (Volunteer Centre, 1989).
45 *Observer*, 2 September 1990.
46 *Guardian*, 14 September 1990.
47 *Volunteers*, no. 73 (Volunteer Centre, May 1990).
48 *Promotion of Volunteering*, cited at note 44.

2 An Uneasy Alliance

1 *Report of the Committee on Local Authority and Allied Personal Social Services* (Seebohm Report) (HMSO, 1968); and *The Voluntary Worker in the Social Services: Report of a Committee Set Up by NCSS and NISW under the Chairmanship of Geraldine M. Aves* (Bedford Square Press, 1969).

2 The Volunteer Centre, *Guidelines for Relationships between Volunteers and Paid Non-Professional Workers* (Volunteer Centre, 1975).

3 *Hansard*, 15 March 1979, cols 714–20.

4 Conservative Central Office, News Service, 211/79.

5 The Volunteer Centre, *Volunteers and Industrial Action: January to March 1979* (unpublished report, 1979).

6 Conservative Central Office, News Service, EE512/79.

7 DHSS, *Health Services Management if Industrial Relations Break Down*, HC(79)20 (DHSS, 1979).

8 *The Times*, 4 January 1980.

9 *Guardian*, 18 July 1980; *The Times*, 17 July 1980.

10 On the establishment of the Supply and Transport Organisation and its operation during the General Strike, see K. Jeffery and P. Hennessy, *States of Emergency: British Governments and Strike Breaking Since 1919* (Routledge, 1983).

11 For a detailed discussion of Emergency Planning under the Attlee administrations, see J. P. Davis Smith, *The Attlee and Churchill Administrations and Industrial Unrest, 1945–55* (Pinter Publishers, 1990).

12 Papers at the Public Records Office (PRO), Kew, CAB 130/16.

13 PRO, CAB 134/178.

14 PRO, CAB 7(47), 16 January 1947.

15 PRO, MT 63/489 and MT 63/488.

16 PRO, CAB 134/176.

17 PRO, Emergencies Committee of Ministers, 23 October 1953, PREM 11/543.

18 J. Boyd-Carpenter, *Way of Life* (Sidgewick & Jackson, 1980), p. 114.

19 *Guardian*, 4 February 1980.

20 *Guardian*, 14 June 1984.

21 *Health and Social Service Journal*, 5 September 1985.

22 *Financial Times*, 6 April 1984.

23 *Guardian*, 13 April 1985.

24 For a discussion of Labour's shifting attitude to the volunteer, see

R. Crossman, 'The role of the volunteer in the modern social service', in A. H. Halsey (ed.), *Tradition in Social Policy* (Blackwell, 1976).

25 Labour Community Action, *Labour and the Voluntary Sector* (Transport and General Workers' Union, 1990).

3 Democracy, Voluntary Action and the Social Welfare Sector in Mainland Europe

1 A. de Tocqueville's work may be approached via the exposition by G. Poggi, *Images of Society: Essays on the Sociological Theories of Tocqueville, Marx and Durkheim* (Oxford University Press, 1972).

2 D. P. Conradt, *The German Polity*, 3rd edn (Longman, 1986).

3 T. Hayes, 'The Church and the voluntary sector in Ireland: brief history and current impact', in *Towards the 21st Century: Challenges for the Voluntary Sector, Proceedings of the Conference of the Association of Voluntary Action Scholars* (Centre for Voluntary Organisation, London School of Economics, 1990), vol. 1.

4 Catholic Truth Society, *The Social Order: The Encyclical Quadragesimo Anno of Pius XI* (Catholic Truth Society, 1931).

5 H. K. Anheir, 'The nonprofit sector in West Germany: definitions and data sources', in *Spring Research Forum*, working papers, 'The nonprofit sector in the United States and abroad: cross-cultural perspectives' (Independent Sector/United Way Strategic Institute, Boston, Mass.,1990). Selected papers published in R. Sumariwalla and K. McCarthy (eds), *The Nonprofit Sector in the United States and Abroad* (Jossey-Bass, San Francisco, 1991).

6 R. Bauer, 'Voluntary welfare associations in Germany and the United States', in *Towards the 21st Century*, vol. 1, cited at note 3.

7 W. Siebel, 'Government/third sector relationships in a comparative perspective: the cases of France and West Germany', *Voluntas*, vol. 1, no. 1 (1990).

8 J. Matzdat, 'On Support for self-help groups at the local level', in S. Humble and J. Unell (eds), *Self-Help in Health and Social Welfare: England and West Germany* (Routledge, 1989).

9 C. Badelt, 'Voluntary action in Austria' (unpublished conference paper, Volunteer Centre, 1978).

10 D. Grunow, 'Why do we need data? Observations on evaluation

research in self-related self-help', in Humble and Unell (eds), *Self-Help in Health and Social Welfare*, cited at note 8.

11 P. Ely, 'Where self-support supports democracy', *Involve: Journal of The Volunteer Centre UK*, no. 70 (February 1990).

12 C. Oldfield, 'Volunteering in West Germany', *Youth Action* (May 1985).

13 J. Hooper, *The Spaniards: A Portrait of the New Spain* (Viking, 1986).

14 D. Sassoon, *Contemporary Italy: Politics, Economics and Society since 1945* (Longman, 1986).

15 S. Pasquinelli, 'Voluntary action in the welfare state: the Italian case', *Nonprofit and Voluntary Sector Quarterly*, vol. 18, no. 4 (winter 1989).

16 J. Montserrat, 'The role of the nonprofit organisations in Spain: trends in contracting-out', in *Towards the 21st Century*, vol. 2, cited at note 3.

17 G. Newton, *The Netherlands: An Historical and Cultural Survey* (Ernest Benn, 1975).

18 Landelijk Steunpunt Vrijwilligerswerk, *National Point of Support Volunteer Work Policy Plan 85/88* (LSV, Utrecht, 1985).

19 H. Kluiver, 'Democracy, rights and NGOs', in *Towards the 21st Century*, vol. 1, cited at note 3.

20 T. Van der Ploeg, 'Changes in the relationship between private organisations and government in the Netherlands', in *Spring Research Forum*, cited at note 5.

21 *National Point of Support Volunteer Work*, cited at note 18.

22 Siebel, 'Government/third sector relationships', cited at note 7.

23 W. Safran, *The French Polity*, 2nd edn (Longman, 1985).

24 EC, *The Extent and Kind of Voluntary Work in the EEC: Questions Surrounding the Relationship between Volunteering and Employment* (Commission of the European Communities, Luxembourg, 1986).

25 Jeanson, quoted in J. Hayward, 'Dissentient France: the counter political culture', in V. Wright (ed.), *Conflict and Consensus in France* (Cass, 1979).

26 D. Duprez, *Prévention de la délinquance et protection judiciaire de la jeunesse* (Centre Lillois d'Etudes et de Recherches Sociologiques et Economiques, Lille, 1987).

27 EC, *The Extent and Kind of Voluntary Work in the EEC*, cited at note 24.

28 P. Ely, 'The new spirit of Dunkirk', *Involve: Journal of The Volunteer Centre UK*, no. 60 (autumn 1986).

29 D. Ferrand-Bechmann, 'Missions, purposes and functions of nonprofit organisations in France', in *Spring Research Forum*, cited at note 5.
30 J. Boli, 'Ties that bind: the nonprofit sector and the state in Sweden', in *Spring Research Forum*, cited at note 5.
31 P. Selle and B. Øymyr, *Explaining Changes in the Population of Voluntary Organisations: Aggregate or Individual Level Data* (Research Centre for Organisation and Management, Bergen, 1990).
32 H. Lorentzen, 'Welfare and values: the adaption of voluntary religious service production to expanding welfare state standards', in *Towards the 21st Century*, vol. 1, cited at note 3.
33 U. Haberman, *Voluntary Work in a Nordic Welfare State* (Socialministeriet, Copenhagen, 1989).
34 A. Gould, *Conflict and Control in Welfare Policy: the Swedish Experience* (Longman, 1988).
35 J. Bugajski and M. Pollack, *East European Fault Lines: Dissent, Opposition and Social Action* (Westview, 1989).
36 T. G. Ash, 'Eastern Europe: après le déluge, nous', *New York Review of Books*, vol. 37, no. 13 (16 August 1990).
37 Bugajski and Pollack, *East European Fault Lines*, cited at note 35.
38 A. Hegelson, 'USSR: the implications of Glasnost and Perestroika?', in B. Munday (ed.), *The Crisis in Welfare: An International Perspective in Social Services and Social Work* (Harvester Wheatsheaf, 1989).
39 H. Hall and J. Ellis, 'The millenium celebrations of 1988 in the USSR', *Religion in Communist Lands*, vol. 16, no. 4 (winter 1988).
40 D. A. Brody and E. T. Boris, 'Philanthropy and charity in the Soviet Union', in *Spring Research Forum*, cited at note 5.
41 J. B. Dunlop, 'The Russian Orthodox Church in the millenium year: what it needs from the Soviet state', *Religion in Communist Lands*, vol. 16, no. 2 (summer 1988).
42 N. Belyaeva, 'Independent sector in the USSR: formation purposes and effects', in *Spring Research Forum*, cited at note 5.

4 What We Know about Volunteering

1 The NOP Survey is reported in Wolfenden, *The Future of Voluntary Organisations* (Croom Helm, 1978); the 1981 Volunteer Centre Survey is reported in Field and Hedges, *National Survey of Volunteering*, cited at note 2; the 1981 General Household Survey

is reported in *OPCS Social Survey*, cited at note 3; the 1987 General Household Survey is reported in Matheson, *General Household Survey 1987*, cited at note 2; the Charities Aid Foundation surveys are reported in *The Charitable Behaviour of the British People* (CAF, 1987), *Charity Household Survey* (CAF, 1988), and *Charity Household Survey* (CAF, 1990); the MORI Survey is reported in *Voluntary Activity: A Survey of Public Attitudes* (Volunteer Centre, 1990). All the surveys have been restricted to Great Britain; none have looked at volunteering in Northern Ireland. However, a survey to be published by The Volunteer Centre UK in 1991 will include Northern Ireland for the first time. Moreover, the survey (apart from the NI element) is a direct replica of the 1981 SCPR/Volunteer Centre survey, enabling us to trace trends in volunteering during the 1980s.

2 For a fuller discussion of the methodological and definitional problems of measuring volunteering, see J. Field and B. Hedges, *A National Survey of Volunteering* (Social and Community Planning Research, 1984), ch. 1; J. Matheson, *General Household Survey 1987: Voluntary Work* (HMSO, 1990), pp. 2–4; and P. Halfpenny, 'Volunteering in Britain', in *Charity Trends 13th Edition* (Charities Aid Foundation, 1990), pp. 36–40.

3 The Volunteer Centre Survey is detailed in Field and Hedges, *National Survey of Volunteering*, cited at note 2; details of the 1981 General Household Survey can be found in *OPCS Social Survey Division Series GHS, No. 11* (HMSO, 1983).

4 Policy Studies Institute, *Voluntary Work and Unemployment* (Manpower Services Commission, 1983).

5 American surveys reviewed in *The Chronicle of Philanthropy* (May 1990), p. 27.

6 Social and Community Planning Research, *On Volunteering: A Qualitative Research Study of Images, Motivations and Experiences* (Volunteer Centre, 1990).

7 The surveys from Belgium and France are reported in Policy Studies Institute, *The Extent and Kind of Voluntary Work in the EEC* (Commission of the European Communities, 1986); the Danish Survey is reported in Merete Watt Boolsen and Helle Holt, *Voluntary Action in Denmark and Britain* (Danish National Institute of Social Research, 1988); the Canadian Survey is reported in Statistics Canada, *Survey of Volunteer Activity* (Statistics Canada, 1988); the survey from the Netherlands is reported in an unpublished paper from the Dutch National Centre for Volunteer Work (Landelijk Steunpunt Vrijwilligerswerk,

1989); the 1985, 1988 and 1990 surveys of volunteering in the United States were all conducted by the Gallup Organization for the Independent Sector and are reported in two reports, *Giving and Volunteering in the United States: Findings from a National Survey* (Independent Sector, 1988, 1990); the 1987 US Survey is detailed in *Volunteering: A National Profile* (Volunteer – The National Center, 1987).

8 MORI, *A Caring Society* (MORI, 1989).

9 Black Perspectives in Volunteering Group, *Black People and Volunteering* (ADVANCE, 1988).

5 Organising and Managing Volunteers

1 MORI, *Voluntary Activity: A Survey of Public Attitudes* (Volunteer Centre, 1990).

2 J. Field and B. Hedges, *A National Survey of Volunteering* (Social and Community Planning Research, 1984).

3 NCVO, *Directions for the Next Decade: Understanding Social and Institutional Trends* (NCVO, 1990).

4 CIPFA, *Comparative Local Authority Statistics 1989, Actuals* (CIPFA, 1990).

5 N. True, *Giving*, Policy Study no. 113 (Centre for Policy Studies, 1990).

6 David McLellan (ed.), *Karl Marx, Selected Writings* (Oxford University Press, 1977).

7 A. Maslow, *Motivation and Personality* (Harper & Row, 1954).

8 F. Herzberg, *Work and the Nature of Man* (World Publishing Co. 1966).

9 D. McGregor, *The Human Side of Enterprise* (Penguin, 1972).

10 Charles Handy, *Understanding Organizations* (Penguin, 1985).

11 Taken from ADVANCE, *Involving Volunteers in an Organisation: Guidelines and Model Policy* (ADVANCE, 1990).

12 Social and Community Planning Research, *On Volunteering: A Qualitative Research Study of Images, Motivations and Experiences* (Volunteer Centre, 1990).

13 Black Perspectives in Volunteering Group, *Black People and Volunteering* (ADVANCE, 1988).

14 Cited at note 12.

15 *A National Survey*, cited at note 2.

16 *Involve Magazine* (February 1985) Involve Magazine is now called *Volunteers* and is published by The Volunteer Centre UK.

17 LVSC, *Voluntary But Not Amateur: A Guide to the Law for Voluntary Organisations and Community Groups* (LVSC, 1990).

18 C. Handy, *Understanding Voluntary Organizations* (Penguin, 1989).

19 ibid.

20 *Caring for People: Community Care in the Next Decade and Beyond*, Cm 849 (HMSO, 1989).

21 L. M. S. Williams and P. A. Cheney, *Counting With Care, A Report of the Kent Volunteer Bureaux Self Monitoring Project* (Volunteer Centre, 1986). See also, Martin Knapp, *The Economics of Volunteering* (Volunteer Centre, 1990).

22 D. Billis, *A Theory of the Voluntary Sector: Implications for Policy and Practice, CVO Working Paper No. 5* (Centre for Voluntary Organisation, LSE, 1989).

23 ibid.

24 ibid.

25 P. Abrams, S. Abrams, R. Humphrey, and R Snaith, *Action for Care* (Volunteer Centre, 1981).

26 ADVANCE, *Equal Opportunities and Volunteering: A Guide to Good Practice* (ADVANCE, 1990).

27 Published by Arrow Press, 1974.

28 ADVANCE, *On the Right Track, a Guide to Finding and Keeping Volunteers*, (ADVANCE, 1988).

29 London Hospital Based Voluntary Services Co-ordinators Group, *A Survey of Voluntary Service Departments in Hospitals* (ADVANCE, 1987).

30 The Volunteer Centre UK, *Guidelines for Relationships between Volunteers and Paid Workers in the Health and Personal Social services* (Volunteer Centre, 1990).

31 ADVANCE, *Equal Opportunities and Volunteering*, cited at note 26.

6 Community Organisations and Voluntary Action

1 David Billis, *Voluntary Sector Management: Research and Practice*, Working Paper 1 (PORTVAC/Centre for Voluntary Organisation, LSE, 1984). Billis has subsequently refined and developed this analysis in *A Theory of the Voluntary Sector: Implications for Policy and Practice*, Working Paper no. 5 (Centre for Voluntary Organisations, LSE, 1989).

2 A full account of the Community Association movement in

Britain on which this section is based is found in Raymond Clarke
et al., Enterprising Neighbours (National Federation of Community Organisations and Community Projects Foundation,
1990).

3 ibid., p. 27.
4 ibid., p. 93.
5 ibid., p. 92.
6 ibid.
7 ibid., p. viii, Foreword by David Donnison.
8 ibid., p. 11.
9 This section is based on Jenny Bentall-Williams, *Anyfing for the
Kids: A Community Development Approach to Youth Work*
(Cambridge House and Talbot, 1984).
10 ibid., p. 45.
11 Peter Tihanyi, *Volunteers, Why They Come and Why They Stay: A
Study of the Motives and Rewards of Volunteers Working in Jewish
Voluntary Organisation Day Centres*, edited by Colin Rochester,
Case Study 1 (Centre for Voluntary Organisation, LSE, April
1991).

7 Black People and Volunteering

1 See J. Field and B. Hedges, *A National Survey of Volunteering*
(Social and Community Planning Research, 1984).
2 MORI, *Voluntary Activity: A Survey of Public Attitudes* (Volunteer
Centre, 1990).
3 The Black Perspectives in Volunteering Group was formed in
1986. The research referred to was funded by the Joseph
Rowntree Memorial Fund and published under the title *Black
People and Volunteering* (ADVANCE, 1988).
4 London Voluntary Service Council, *Bridges: A Directory of
African, Afro-Caribbean, Asian, Latin American and Mediterranean
Community Groups in Greater London* (LVSC, 1988).
5 The Resource Unit to Promote Black Volunteering can be
contacted at Unit 117–119, Brixton Enterprise Centre, 444
Brixton Road, London SW9 9ES, tel. 071-738 3462.
6 For a general guide on equal opportunities and volunteering,
including the legal aspects, I recommend, *Equal Opportunities and
Volunteering: A Guide to Good Practice* (ADVANCE, 1990).
7 The Volunteer Centre UK, *Encouraging Signs?* (Volunteer Centre,
1991).

8 For a review of recent developments see Rifat Wahhab, *Section 11 – For Better or Worse* (Organisation Development Unit, NCVO, Briefing Note, February 1991). See also NCVO and NAREC, *Section 11 – Funding for Black and Ethnic Minorities? Guidance Notes for Voluntary Groups* (NCVO, 1991).

9 Home Office, *Profiting from Partnership: Efficiency Scrutiny of Government Funding of the Voluntary Sector* (HMSO, 1990). See, in particular, paras 3.6.8 to 3.6.12 with regard to volunteering, and ethnic involvement in volunteering.

8 Volunteers as Advocates

1 William Bingley *et. al., Advocacy Information Pack* (Good Practices in Mental Health, 1986).

2 B. Crawley, *The Growing Voice: A Survey of Self-Advocacy Groups in Adult Training Centres and Hospitals in Great Britain* (Campaign for People with Mental Handicaps, 1988).

3 A. Forrest, *Citizen Advocacy: Including the Excluded* (Sheffied Advocacy Project, 1986).

The following publications were also consulted:

Butler, K., Carr, S., and Sullivan, F., *Citizen Advocacy: A Powerful Partnership* (National Citizen Advocacy, 1988).

Lawrence, R., *Volunteers as Advocates* (Volunteer Centre, 1982).

Rankin, M., *Advocacy: Some Perspectives for the Nineties: A Conference Report* (Volunteer Centre, 1989).

Willis, E., *Marginalisation: Volunteering as a Strategy against Exclusion* (Volunteer Centre, 1987).

Acknowledgement is also made to Marjorie Arthurs for thoughts on advocacy and befriending.

9 Self-Help Groups: Is there Room for Volunteers?

1 Stephen Hatch and Teresa Hinton, *Self-Help in Practice: A Study of Contact-a-Family, Community Work and Family Support* (Policy Studies Institute, 1986).

2 Samual Smiles, *Self-Help: With Illustrations of Character, Conduct and Perseverance* (1859; Penguin, 1958).

3 P. Kropotkin, *Mutual Aid: A Factor of Evolution* (1914; Garland, New York, 1972).
4 See Jill Vincent, *Constraints on the Stability and Longevity of Self-Help Groups in the Field of Health Care* (Centre for Research in Social Policy, Loughborough University, 1986).
5 Gareth H. Williams, 'Hope for the humblest? The role of self-help in chronic illness: the case of ankylosing spondylitis', *Sociology of Illness and Health*, vol. 11, no. 2 (June 1989).
6 G. Lindenfield, 'Self-help and mental health', *MASH (Mutual Aid and Self-Help)*, no. 7 (spring 1988).
7 Julia Warren and Joyce Walls, 'Women and Tranquillisers Group', *MASH*, no. 12 (summer 1989).
8 *Notes on a National Self-Help Support Centre Conference March 1990*.
9 Steve Dowson, 'CMH: Working with people with learning difficulties', *MASH*, no. 14 (winter 1989).
10 Department of Health, *Working for Patients*, Cm 555 (HMSO), 1989).
11 Department of Health, *Caring for People: Community Care in the Next Decade and Beyond*, Cm 849 (HMSO, 1989).

Useful Names and Addresses

The following self-help groups are mentioned in this chapter. For further help about self-help, please contact the National Self-Help Support Centre, National Council for Voluntary Organisations, 26 Bedford Square, London WC1B 3HU, tel. 071-636 4066.

Alcohol Advice Centre
44 Vicar lane
Chesterfield S40 1PX
Tel. 0246-204344.

Contact-a-Family
16 Strutton Ground
London SW1P 2HP
Tel. 071-222 2695.

Black Carers Support Group
Annie Wood Resource Centre
129 Alma Way
Lozells
Birmingham B19 2LS
Tel. 021-554 7137.

Mind Your Self
157 Woodhouse Lane
Leeds LS2 3ED
Tel. 0532-430918.

People First
Oxford House
Derbyshire Street
London E2 6HG
Tel. 071-739 3890.

Spectrum
See note below.

Values Into Action
Oxford House
Derbyshire Street
London E2 6HG
Tel. 071-729 5436.

Womankind
76 Colston Street
Bristol BS1 5BB
Tel. 0272-252507.

Note: Spectrum no longer exists, but out of the Spectrum idea other groups have now been formed. The umbrella organisation for these is the Federation of West Derbyshire Mental Health Support Groups, Ernest Bailey Community Centre, New Street, Matlock DE4 3FE. Tel. 0629-580935.

Index

Related Titles from NCVO Publications

Active Citizens
New Voices and Values
Nick Fielding, Gillian Reeve and Margaret Simey

This book aims to introduce some plain thinking into the rhetoric of public announcements about active citizenship. First, Margaret Simey looks at how volunteering has developed since the beginning of the century. This is followed by a series of interviews with present-day active citizens whose work is both representative and inspirational. The final part looks to the future and the way ahead for the voluntary sector.

The Gentle Art of Listening
Counselling Skills for Volunteers
Janet K. Ford and Philippa Merriman

Written for all those who work, or may be thinking of working, as volunteer counsellors or befrienders, this book covers practical as well as emotional questions and examines what is involved. '...one of the best handbooks on listening skills I have read'. Hugh Harrison, *Care Weekly*.

For further details, please contact the NCVO Publications Sales Office, NCVO, 26 Bedford Square, London WC1B 3HU, telephone 071-636 4066 ext 2212.

The Voluntary Agencies Directory 1991

The Social Activists' Bible

NCVO's directory of voluntary agencies is the standard reference work for anyone who cares about helping the community. It lists nearly 2,000 leading voluntary agencies, ranging from small, specialist self-help groups to long-established national charities. It gives concise, up-to-date descriptions of their aims and activities with details of

charitable status	local branches
volunteer participation	membership
trading activities	staffing

A list of useful addresses includes professional and public advisory bodies concerned with voluntary action; a classified index and quick reference list of acronyms and abbreviations give easy access to entries.

There is extensive coverage of groups concerned with women's issues, minority rights, self-help, community development and leisure activities, environment and conservation, campaigning and consumer affairs.

Voluntary agencies play an important part in making the world a better place to live in. This NCVO directory is the essential guide to their work.

'If you buy only one directory of voluntary agencies, buy this one and buy it every year.' *Health Libraries Review*

'...an essential working tool.' *Environment Now*

£10.95

BSP Practical Guides

Titles in the series:

All books are available through bookshops and can be purchased from NCVO Reception during office hours. In case of difficulty books can be ordered by post direct from Plymbridge Distributors Ltd, Estover Road, Plymouth PL6 7PZ (tel. 0752-705251) adding 12½% to total value of order for post and packing (minimum 45p).

Titles in the **BSP Survival Handbooks** series:

Jane Brotchie
Help at Hand: The Home Carers' Survival Guide

Shirley Cooklin
From Arrest to Release: The Inside/Outside Survival Guide

Neil Davidson
Boys Will Be...? Sex Education and Young Men

Janet K. Ford and Philippa Merriman
The Gentle Art of Listening: Counselling Skills for Volunteers

Gingerbread/CEDC
Just Me and the Kids: A Manual for Lone Parents

Sandra Horley
Love and Pain: A Survival Handbook for Women

Tony Lake and Fran Acheson
Room to Listen, Room to Talk: A Beginner's Guide to Analysis, Therapy and Counselling

Jacquelynn Luben
Cot Deaths: Coping with Sudden Infant Death Syndrome

Malcolm Macourt
How Can We Help You? Information, Advice and Counselling for Gay Men and Lesbians

In addition to this book **NCVO Publications** (including Bedford Square Press) publishes books and reports on a range of current voluntary sector and social issues. BSP series include Survival Handbooks, Community Action, Practical Guides, Society Today, Directories, Reports, Organisation and Management, and Fundraising.

If you would like to receive a copy of the current stocklist, or further details of any title, please complete the coupon below and forward it to:

> Sales Department
> NCVO Publications
> 26 Bedford Square
> London WC1B 3HU
>
> Tel: 071-636 4066 (x2212)

☐ Please send me your latest catalogue/booklist (please tick)

☐ Please send me further details of the following titles:

1. _____

2. _____

3. _____

4. _____

☐ Please add my name to your regular mailing list. My areas of interest are (please state):

_____

NAME: _____

ADDRESS: _____

_____

_____Post code: _____

You may photocopy this page.   Volsoc

The Women's Directory
Compiled by Fiona Macdonald

The Women's Directory will enable women who wish to make contact with others - whether for social, cultural, sporting, charitable, self-help or political purposes - to locate and identify suitable groups and organisations. It refers women to appropriate 'umbrella' bodies, whether voluntary, local-government-based or state funded, and gives other sources of information about women's activities, including relevant magazines and journals, publishers and bookshops. Information is presented in an accessible, simple-to-follow format, with symbols used to give additional information.

£6.95